Word Weaving

The Cheshire Prize for Literature Anthologies

Prize Flights: Stories from the Cheshire Prize for
Literature 2003; edited by Ashley Chantler

Life Lines: Poems from the Cheshire Prize for
Literature 2004; edited by Ashley Chantler

Word Weaving

*Stories and Poems for Children
from the Cheshire Prize for
Literature
2005*

Edited by Jaki Brien

*Introduction
by
Michael Morpurgo*

Chester Academic Press

First published 2006
by Chester Academic Press
University of Chester
Parkgate Road
Chester CH1 4BJ

Printed and bound in the UK by the
Learning Resources Print Unit,
University of Chester
Cover designed by the
Learning Resources Graphics Team,
University of Chester

A catalogue record for this book is available
from the British Library

CONTENTS

Word Weaving

THE CONTRIBUTORS

Sheila M. Blackburn has always been a keen writer. As a primary school teacher, she is keen to foster a love of reading and writing in children, particularly reluctant readers, and likes to write a lot of her own material. Her work includes 12 stories about football-mad Sam; these will soon be followed by six stories about Stewie Scraps, who loves making things from junk. She has also had several adult short stories published in *My Weekly* magazine.

David Brazier, a keen diver with a lifelong love of the sea, has spent half his life in the Middle East, where he was fortunate enough to witness turtles digging their nests and laying their eggs many times and to protect turtle hatchlings during their desperate dash to the sea. "Leatherback" was hatched from the memory of those wonderful encounters.

Nick Buchanan lectures in Graphic Design and delivers National Trainings. He is grateful to Dot and Mike, who gave him a childhood in which questions were never squashed with "answers." He likes the sound of fresh fallen snow squeaking underfoot, the look of sunlight underwater and the glide of a ballpoint pen on the sole of his slippers. He is married with two sons and lives on the Wirral.

I. E. Challender graduated in Ancient and Medieval History from the University of London, and studied at the Institute of Archaeology. She has had a lifelong fascination with the past. Her four children, and grandchildren, provided a captive audience for her storytelling and now she is delighted the story in this book has managed to escape to a wider public.

Merle Colborne was born in South Africa and has recently returned to Chester, where she first met her husband. She is currently working on her grand opus - an old narrowboat she cycles out to almost daily. Journalist, copywriter, columnist, award-winning feature writer, Merle has published short stories and a critically acclaimed novella and is looking for an enthusiastic agent/publisher for her new novel, *The Beautiful Bleeding Icebergs*.

David Diggory was born in Manchester and moved with his family to live in Upton-by-Chester in the early 1960s. He was educated at Liverpool Polytechnic, the College of Law and Dundee University. Subsequently, he lived in London and Oslo. He likes cycling and walking.

Tricia Durdey is a writer, movement artist, and Pilates teacher. She lived in the city of Chester for eighteen years, but now lives with her family in the Derbyshire hills. She is at present working on a novel for young adults about disability and dancing, set in Amsterdam during the Nazi occupation.

Vanessa Greatorex is a freelance writer and historian whose children are fascinated by pirates. With them in mind, she rebelliously dashed off *The Reluctant Cabin Boy* when she was supposed to be concentrating on a dissertation about Shotwick Churchyard. "I was sick of writing footnotes and wanted to have a go at blending historical fact with fiction," she says. "After being shackled by academic constraints, writing about subversive characters was gloriously liberating."

Word Weaving

Liz Haigh is a mother of two young children; she lives and works in Chester. She loves reading and is a member of a local reading circle. Her writing aspirations have until now been limited to a passion for writing poetry. Liz has had a couple of her poems published, but this is her first venture into the world of short stories.

Libby Harris moved north from Swansea with her husband and two daughters ten years ago, and has been lucky enough to live in central Chester for the last six years. She is a distance tutor in European Union Law for a College in Bedford, and escapes into novels as often as possible.

Gary Hayden is 41 years old. He has spent most of his life in Halton, and most of his working life teaching in Runcorn primary schools. Last year he moved to Singapore where his wife Wendy teaches in an international school. He now works full-time as a freelance writer (see www.garyhayden.co.uk). "Thursday Afternoon Showdown" is his first children's story.

D. K. Jones was born in Mumbles, near Swansea, in 1920. He served in World War Two and was taken prisoner near Tunis in December 1942, but escaped from three Italian prisoner of war camps (the third time successfully) and was home for Christmas in 1943. After the War, he became Founder/Secretary of the Army POW Escape Club, while working for the Prison Service and HM Customs & Excise. He and his wife Edith live in Chester and have two daughters, four grandchildren and eight great-grandchildren.

Pauline Leung studied at Étienne Decroux's École de Mime in Paris before setting up her own puppet company, based on mime and dance. Pauline is qualified in the holistic therapies (massage, aromatherapy, reflexology and reiki). She enjoys writing short stories and was runner-up in *The Mail on Sunday* writing competition, 2005. She is married with one son, Richard.

Jane Mack has written poetry since she was nine and goes to various local writers' and poetry groups. She studied French at Manchester University, and more recently did an MPhil on Laurie Lee. She is a tutor in Italian at West Cheshire College and English Literature with the WEA. She is also a Green Badge Guide for Chester, where she has lived with her family for over twenty years.

John Mead graduated from Manchester Metroplitan University last summer with a Writing degree, and the Cheshire Prize for Literature offered a good opportunity for him to showcase his work to a wider audience. Unfortunately, this story is based on his own experience of his best friend's battle with cancer. He has found the writing of it a cathartic and at times difficult process.

Sheila Powell is fifty-eight, married with two sons. She has been writing for many years and has sold a few articles and stories. Losing herself in writing gives her the same pleasure she enjoyed as a child, reading her favourite books. When not writing, she is teaching, working in a library, dog-walking, gardening and being a housewife, all of which she enjoys enormously.

Eleanor Pownall was born in Cheshire in 1975. She began writing seriously after completing a travel writing course at the University of Liverpool and has since written for *Cumbria* magazine. She is new to children's fiction and has found inspiration in her family history and the Cheshire landscape. Eleanor loves the rich diversity of the county: the beautiful countryside, historical landmarks, its industry, estuaries and borderlands.

Maggie Spooner is a member of the Wilmslow Writers' Group. She has had some success with children's stories, but writes mainly poetry, particularly with nature or conservation as its theme. In 2004, she was the winner of The BBC Wildlife Magazine's competition for Poet of the Year.

Juliet Watkinson studied Art and English at university in Wales and then took a professional course in Theatre Design at English National Opera. She first came to Chester to be Head of Design at the Gateway Theatre and Chester has remained her home. "Occhi" was her first piece of writing for children, but she has now written the script for "The Swap", a short video drama about children's life on the Shropshire canal in the early 1950s. It will soon be shown in Cheshire primary schools.

David Whitley is 21. He is from Chester, having until recently attended the King's School. He is currently reading English at Corpus Christi College, Oxford, where he is daily humbled by the magnificence of the writers that he studies. He was shortlisted for the Fidler Award for first time children's writers in 2001, but this is his first published work. He has a small dream that it will not be his last.

Jaki Brien (editor) is a lecturer in the School of Education at the University of Chester. She contributes to several programmes and particularly enjoys teaching courses on writing for teachers and specialist modules on children's literature on both undergraduate and Masters' programmes. She has written many short stories for educational publishers, but retains the ambition of writing something which children will actually choose to read.

INTRODUCTION

Everyone of you who entered the Cheshire Prize for Literature will know the blank page or the blank screen. There it is, staring back at you, and the more you stare back the emptier it gets, the more frightening it gets. We have all been there, from Shakespeare to Stevenson, Hardy to Hughes, Dickens to Dahl. Like them, like you, like me – we've all found a way to let our writing flow. For what it's worth, here's my way.

I have been very lucky. I have had a very varied and interesting life – over 60 years of it. My childhood was spent in the country, by the sea, in a big city. I went to day school, to boarding school, I had great teachers and cruel teachers. I had a particular interest in history and geography, oh yes, and in rugby and cricket. I didn't read much, but I read widely, from comics to classics. When I grew up, I lived here, there and everywhere. I became a soldier, a teacher, a farmer. I was husband, father, grandfather. I was a teenager, a young man, a middle-aged man, and now an older middle-aged man. I've travelled all over the world. I love islands in particular. I've met lots of interesting people, in trains, in buses, on airplanes. I've known writers and businessmen and artists, farmers, foresters, and publishers and all sorts of people. And all this time, I've been looking, listening, feeling my way, learning. I've been gathering all this into my memory for the last 60 years

Once the seed for my story is planted in my brain, I dream it out: (Note – I still haven't gone anywhere near a blank piece of paper.) For days, weeks, months, years, it grows into a story inside my head. I don't force it or mould it but, by going back to my dream, I allow it to take root. I do research of all kinds to help it grow, to add richness.

And all the while I'm coming to believe in my story, to have confidence in it.

When I begin to write, I don't write, rather I speak the words down on to the page. I speak it down, fast. I don't worry about what it looks like, spelling, punctuation, all that stuff. All that can come later. I just get it down. I let it flow.

Then I read it through, read it out loud, listen to it, hear my story telling itself to me for the first time. I correct it, tweak it, fiddle with it, till I'm happy.

Quite why I've chosen in the introduction of this book to talk about how I go about making stories, I don't know, when it's quite clear to me that the 20 wonderful writers in this book need no advice from me. I did it, though, in solidarity, knowing as they do what it takes to make a story. Bravo to them! Bravo to the Cheshire Prize for Literature.

EDITOR'S FOREWORD

Word Weaving is a collection of the best entries for the 2005 Cheshire Prize for Literature competition. This prize, which was instigated by John Richards, the former High Sheriff of the county, seeks to give a voice to writers with a link to Cheshire and to celebrate their work. It receives generous sponsorship from the MBNA Foundation and is administered by the University of Chester.

In her inaugural speech as the new Children's Laureate, Jacqueline Wilson asserted that "this is a new golden age of children's literature." It was in this climate of intense interest in all aspects of children's reading that it was decided that the 2005 Cheshire Prize for Literature should be for an original and previously unpublished piece of writing for children.

The winner of the First Prize was David Whitley, for "The Substitute" and the two Runners-Up Prizes were won by Tricia Durdey, for "The Sea Pearl", and Sheila Powell, for "The Whisper". Additionally, The School of Education at the University of Chester awarded a Prize for the entry which most impressed a panel of young advisory judges. This was won by John Mead, for "I Know Certain Things". The other entries on the final short list were Nick Buchanan's "The Worm, the Telly and the Nightingale" and "Romany" by Libby Harris.

All the entries published here certainly indicate that this is a "golden age". Each author has woven words together with sensitive dexterity to create something original and beautiful. These are pieces which can lure children into a love of reading and, like all good children's literature, can be read with pleasure and admiration by adults.

I must thank the judges: Professor Henry Pearson from the University of Chester, John Scrivener (Chairman of the Chester Literature Festival) and Diane Tibbetts (English Advisor for Cheshire) as well as the panel of young judges, for their informed, thoughtful enthusiasm throughout the pleasurable process of sifting through 140 entries. I must also thank the former Children's Laureate, Michael Morpurgo, for his valuable contribution to the final stages of the judging. Thanks are also due to Diane Dennis and Peter Williams for their splendid work in designing and publishing this book. Finally, I must thank Bill Hughes for his efficient organisation of the whole competition and for his championing of children's literature.

In 2006, the Cheshire Prize for Literature will, as in 2003, be for a short story and we hope to publish a selection of the best pieces, including the prize winners, in a similar anthology next year.

THE SUBSTITUTE

David Whitley

We never mentioned him.

The first time he came, I was rushed away. All I remember was the swish of Mum's skirts, hiding him from view. Dad never shouted, not at me, but his voice boomed at the man that night. I couldn't sleep. I crept out after dark to see if the man was still there. The wind didn't leave even a footprint in the dust.

The next year, he came again. This time I peered at him from behind the bales of hay. His feet were bleeding from the road. He asked for me, calling me "the boy." Dad sent him away. Every time, it was the same.

I asked Mum why he wanted me. She kissed me, but said nothing. Later, when Mum was putting me to bed, I asked her why he couldn't stay, at least to rest. We never had any visitors. Mum said that Granddad wouldn't let him. We never argued with Granddad. I wondered if that was what he had done. Mum said it was something much worse.

When I was thirteen, they gave me a word for it: "murderer." Even before they explained what it meant, the word was different from any other I had heard: sharp-edged, dangerous. I went to sit by the stone under the tree, the stone where my brother's name was carved. My brother was dead. He had always been dead, and this was the man who had killed him. He wanted to see me, and I didn't know why.

At night, I used to imagine what he'd do if he found me on my own. Would he kill me? Would I kick and fight back, and kill him? Granddad had forbidden that too. No, I wanted to talk to him. I wanted to know.

I had my chance the next month. Mum and Dad were out in the field, getting in the harvest. Not large, just for us, but enough to send them out of sight over the hill. I felt his gaze upon me. I turned. He stood there, shoulders square against the sun, face in shadow. I was feeding one of the goats, my hand stroking its head. Unmoving, he stared at that hand. I felt like running, shouting, screaming for my parents to come back, to chase him away like they had so many times before.

Instead, I let go of the goat, and went over to a bucket in the corner, fresh drawn from the well.

"Would you like a drink?" I said, trying to sound casual. My voice rattled in my dry throat.

"Yes," he said. I was surprised. His voice was not a killer's; it didn't roar like a lion's. It was just a voice: weary, quiet and deep.

I filled a little wooden cup. The water trembled with my hand, but I made myself stop. Looking at the ground, ready for any tiny movement, I held the cup out to him at arm's length. I felt his fingers brush mine as he took it from me. They were chapped and broken from the heat. There was blood, but I could see it was his own. I heard him raise the cup to his lips and drink. He gave it back, empty. I filled it again. This time, he stared for a moment into the water, and I looked too, at his reflection. Our eyes met in the water and I flicked my gaze away. I thought I should have been able to see it in his eyes. Perhaps the water distorted them, made them seem more human. He drank, dropping the cup in the dust.

"Thank you," he said to the air beside my head. "What's your name?"

"Seth," I said. He grimaced.

"It makes sense," he muttered. "Know what that means?"

"Appointed," I replied. I knew what it meant. Mum

2

had told me that so often, reminded me why I had my name. I was appointed, I had a duty. I was a substitute for him, for my dead brother.

"Where is he?" the murderer asked. I noticed for the first time that he was carrying something in his hand - a bundle of sheepskin, tied with string. I pointed to the tree, and he walked away, out of sight. I bent over to pick up the little wooden cup. As my hands closed around it, I heard the sound of Dad's footsteps. He was coming back. I stopped breathing, holding the cup tight, expecting it to shriek out that the murderer was here, that it had touched a murderer's hands and mouth.

Dad didn't even look at me. He passed by, picked up a tool, and walked back over the hill. I went inside and threw the cup into the fire, burning away the killer's breath.

I found him, kneeling on the ground in front of my brother's stone. His hands hovered near it, not touching. In front of him lay the bundle.

"Why did you kill him?" I asked. I thought it would come out as an accusation, filled with hatred or fury. But I had never known my brother, and it was just a question. I sounded like a little child again.

"I've forgotten," he said, hands dropping to his side. "Not what I did. I'm reminded of that every day." He looked up at me then, the first and last time our eyes met. "I can't remember why."

"Dad said that you were jealous of him," I said, breaking his gaze, moving behind him.

"Was that it?" His voice was hollow.

"He said it started as a competition. That you both wanted to please Grandfather, but no matter what you did, Grandfather always liked him better than you."

"If you know, why are you asking?" he said, not turning round.

3

"I needed to know the truth."

He didn't respond. I wanted so much to grab him, to shake him, to demand. But I stood over him, hardly moving, waiting. He began to undo the package he had brought, peeling it open.

"It was so easy." He spoke to the stone, never to me. "He was standing there, just feeding his goats. Dad said I had to look after him. I'd come out to fetch him for dinner. He said to wait a few minutes. I stood. I thought. My fingers closed around it before I knew what it was."

The package was open; he lifted out the jawbone of an animal, whitened with age. "This is the truth," he said, raising it over his head. "I'll never know what I was feeling, except that I was going to do it." His arm tensed. "I struck him once. Just once. And it was done." He swung his hand forward, as if to bring it crushing down on my brother's gravestone. I stopped him. I caught the jawbone and held it back. He let go, his arm falling back to his side. "Dad lost both his sons that day. That's the only truth I know."

I stood over him; now the jawbone was in my hand. The weapon. I thought about swinging it over my head. I thought about avenging my brother.

I didn't. This was my brother too.

"I was the first born," he said, as he got to his feet, still looking away. "Are you his substitute or mine, Seth?"

I looked at the weapon in my hands, and held it out to him, keeping my fingers closed around it. Showing, not offering.

"Neither," I said. He reached forward, stopped, and nodded. Then he turned, and began to walk away.

"Why did you want to see me?" I called after him. He didn't look back.

"To see who you were, brother," he said, walking on; "And to show you who I am." I watched him go.

4

The Substitute

A year later, I found his body beside the sheepfold. His lips were cracked; he looked as if he had died of thirst. He must have been found on the road and brought there. There were the footsteps of men in the dust.

I asked Grandfather if we could bury him next to his victim. We thought he would refuse, but Grandfather said that it was fitting. We never question him.

I carved the stone myself. It only bears one word, his name. I chipped it away with the jawbone. Then I buried it between them.

I still go to those graves, side-by-side under the tree. Mother and Father went there once, after he was buried. I wish they could forgive. I wish I could. Perhaps, one day, I too will lie beside them, the third brother. I doubt it. I was not made for their story. I am not Cain, I did not strike. I am not Abel, I was not struck. I am Seth. I did neither. I remember. Grandfather tells me that is my purpose: to remember, to know.

I am my brothers' keeper.

I KNOW CERTAIN THINGS

John Mead

Dedicated to Tom Jordan

Before

I know certain things.

I know that the sound of wind whistling through trees is similar to the sound of waves crashing on rocks. I know that the world is round, even though the ground is flat. I know my ten times tables, because all you have to do is add a zero on to the number you are multiplying. I know the name of the Prime Minister and where he lives. And I know that my friend Tom is very ill.

There are also certain things that I don't know. I don't know why grown-ups argue and go to war. I don't know why the sea tastes salty. I don't know why cows sit down before it rains. I don't know where the moon goes in the daytime. And I don't know if Tom is ever going to get better.

After

Tom is my best friend in the whole world. His favourite four things are football, chess, monopoly and peanut butter. I know this off by heart because Tom and I tell each other everything. We know all there is to know about each other. He knows that I'm scared of small dogs, because I don't like the way you can feel their bones through their fur; and I know that he sometimes picks his nose and eats it when he thinks no one is watching. He knows about my secret hiding place under my bed, where I keep my pocket money, and I know that Tom still sleeps with a light outside his door, because he likes to see it creeping in through the cracks in the door frame. There is very little that we keep to ourselves; so when Tom got a disease called cancer, we both went through it together.

Most people think that you can only get cancer when you get old, but that's not true. Tom was eight when he found out that he had cancer, and at the time neither of us really knew what it meant. I'd heard of cancer before, but I never really understood what it was. I used to think it was like catching a cold or having a temperature, but I soon realised it was much more serious than that.

I remember the day that Tom told me he had cancer. He had come round after school to play football against the fence outside my back garden, and we were eating our dinner when he said, "John, I'm poorly."

So I said, "What's the matter? You look fine to me," because I thought he was going to say that he'd hurt himself playing football earlier.

And he said, "My mum says I might have a cancer," and then he just carried on eating chips and beans as if that was that and we'd never have to mention it again. And because he said it in this way, I thought that it couldn't be that bad after all and didn't mention it until teatime a few days later, when I was watching television with Mum and Dad.

"Tom said he might have a cancer." It was only when they stopped eating and put their plates down and started asking me questions that I started to realise it was actually quite serious. And they turned *Coronation Street* off as well, even though it's their favourite programme in the whole world.

Word Weaving

Cancer is not a nice thing. It's a growth which eats away inside you. Sometimes it grows on bones, and sometimes it grows on muscles. Most people never have it, but Tom was very unlucky, and he got it in a bone in his left leg, just below his knee. Pretty much as soon as he was told he had cancer, he was told he had to try to make it go away; because if you leave it, it will get worse and worse.

A week after Tom had told me at the dinner table, I went to see him in hospital for the first time. It was a Thursday afternoon and I was excited, because I had been given permission to leave school early. But on the way to the hospital, my excitement was replaced by a funny feeling that made me uneasy. It felt as if there was a light bulb in my belly, and lots of little moths were flickering and fluttering around it. I'd been to hospital twice before - when I was born and when my friend Andy had his tonsils out last year - but this time felt new and scary, because I didn't know what to expect.

I held my mum's hand as we walked through the wide corridors until we came to Ward Number 23, where Tom was staying. The ward smelt sickly and warm, like the inside of a greenhouse on a summer's evening. Tom was sitting up in his bed at the far end of the ward, next to a huge window. I smiled when I saw him, even though I could still feel the moths tickling the insides of my belly. Tom smiled back and reached out to me with his hand. I didn't really know what he wanted me to do, so I just grabbed it and held it for a second before letting it fall back to his side. His hand had felt all cold and wrinkly, as if he'd been out walking in winter without gloves on. I sat on the chair by the bed and looked at the floor. I felt all shy, as if I was in a room with a stranger, and not my best friend.

I Know Certain Things

When someone has cancer, they have special medicine to try to make it go away. This medicine is put into their body to wash away the bad blood cells that have made the person poorly. Sometimes the medicine has funny effects, like making the person's hair fall out and making them look thinner.

The visits continued week after week after week. By the time Tom had finished his first set of treatment, I knew all of the staff on his ward by name. Sometimes I found it hard to know what to say to Tom, and sometimes my words came easily. After the first three weeks of Tom's stay in hospital, his hair started to fall out. It's strange, because even though I'd been told how serious it all was, it was only when I saw Tom without any hair for the first time that it really began to sink in. And it scared me. It even got to the point that I would dread visiting time, because I knew it would make me upset to see him looking so small and helpless.

One day, I felt like crying as soon as I saw him, but I managed to smile and talk about other things, like football stickers and penny chews, while we played monopoly. And then, when I was leaving, I went straight to the toilets at the end of Tom's ward and locked myself in and cried and cried, until I thought I was going to shrivel up. But mum says it's good to cry sometimes, because it lets the bad feelings out of your body and it makes you ready for tomorrow's challenges.

Three months later, I went to see Tom on a rainy Thursday afternoon, with Mum. I can still remember the way my new trainers squeaked on the shiny floor. When we reached Tom, he seemed to look a bit brighter than normal, so I asked him how he was and he said, "Guess what? The doctors told me the cancer is nearly gone," and when he said this he was nearly laughing, and I remember thinking that it seemed like a long time since I had last heard Tom laugh. And then I looked at him and I didn't know how to react. I started laughing too and reached out to hold Tom's hand; but when I touched it, it still felt cold and clammy and I suddenly felt like crying again. Tears started to run down my face, and when Tom saw me his laughter turned to tears too. And there we were, two friends with the best possible news, both crying like babies without knowing why.

And now I look back on what Tom went through, and what I went through too, and it makes me feel happy, even though it was a horrible time. And I know that might sound funny to you, so let me explain. I feel as though I've been asleep and I've had a terrible nightmare. But now I'm awake, and even though I can still remember how scary the nightmare was, I know that it's over, and I know that it's made me realise how precious life is. Now I just want to start the next chapter of my life. And I know that Tom thinks the same way, because he's sitting next to me now, smiling.

THE SEA PEARL

Tricia Durdey

"Something is going to happen tonight," Molly whispered to herself, as she lay in bed, gazing at the moon over the sea. Downstairs, the grown-ups discussed important things behind closed doors. She wasn't allowed to go to her mother. Instead, her grandmother tucked her in and kissed her goodnight, forgetting to bring her a mug of hot chocolate and a biscuit. Molly did not think it was because of the new baby who was coming in September, as it was still only August. She shivered. It was like waiting for the storms that came every winter over the sea, listening to the wind howling and the waves crashing on the sand; only tonight the sea was calm.

"Something is going to happen. I know." She felt so alone that she couldn't sleep. She looked around at all the familiar things in her room. There were the brown bears and their shadows in the corner, the huge black wardrobe by the door and her wooden chair with the nameless china doll beside the bed. But nothing was the same as before. There were secrets in the house now. She slipped out of bed and stood on the chest to gaze out of the window. The moon was her friend and tonight his face was full and bright. He made a track of golden light across the sea, reaching right into the room.

"What shall I do?" she asked him. "What's going to happen?" She pressed her face against the glass and listened hard.

Sometimes Molly could hear echoes from the City of Shells far beneath the sea. She could hear bells chiming now, a low dong, dong, dong, under the whooshing sound of the waves.

11

"Come now, come now," they called.

She imagined the pearly walls and turrets under the sea, gleaming with all the colours of the rainbow, the gardens full of amber sea flowers, and the silver fish darting from the shelter of rocks.

She put on her slippers and quietly opened her door. She stepped over the floorboard that creaked on the landing and ran down the backstairs, through the kitchen door, to the beach. The cold sand tickled her toes.

"Come now," said the echoing bells.

"Come now," said the moon, and she stepped on to the track he made for her across the black sea.

At once, the cold water swallowed her up. She gasped and reached out her arms to save herself. Then she was swirling and falling. She had never known before that the sea whirled like the wind, catching at her hair and her nightdress, filling her mouth with wet sand. And yet she was not afraid. She lifted her head to follow the shaft of moonlight, and then she was swimming through liquid gold, warm as a summer night.

A shoal of fish, striped silver and pink, flickered by.

"Come with us," said a fish who was slower than the rest. "We are travelling to the Mother of the Sea." Molly took hold of his tail and he swept her through chasms and caves, past a garden of starfish and a herd of green sea horses, their bellies swollen with babies.

Suddenly, the sea turned dark and Molly felt the fish slip away from her grasp. She was alone in a forest of seaweed, and a shower of black sea snakes darted towards her, sliding against her skin, showing their fangs.

"Help me," she called, but all she heard was the echo of her own voice, and the soft shushing of snakes.

"Where are you swimming?"

"To the Mother of the Sea," she answered, as she tried to weave her way past them.

"To pass, you must give us the silver band on your wrist and the dress on your body." They jabbed at her with their heads.

"But then I'll have nothing left."

"Yes," they hissed, "this is so."

And because Molly knew she had no choice but to swim on, she wriggled her silver bracelet from her arm and her nightdress over her head, and the snakes' mouths opened and swallowed them away.

Although she was cold and alone now, Molly groped her way forward along the sandy seabed. Suddenly, she felt a cold hand grasp her own. She pulled away, but it held on fast.

"Help me."

Was it her voice, or another's? She looked down and saw a tiny child, with a fish's tail.

"Who are you; where are you going?" she asked.

"I cannot go forward, and yet I must go on. I have lost my mother, and I'm too tired to swim any longer."

Because she could not bear to leave the sea-child alone, Molly gathered him up. He wrapped his fishy tail around her waist and clasped her neck with his arms. Now her back ached as she crawled, and his fingers dug into her neck.

"Everything will be all right when we reach the Mother of the Sea," he sang, and the sound of his sweet voice gave her courage.

They came to the gates of a palace. The posts were two huge fishtails carved in marble, inlaid with pearl and jet and aquamarine, and between them a shark yawned, his teeth glistening, ready to gnash Molly and the sea-child to pieces and eat them.

"Why should I let you through?" he roared, as Molly cowered behind a rock, the sea-child shivering in her arms.

"Because I am brave," she whispered, though she did not feel brave.

"Show me then how brave you are."

Molly knew she could not go back, and now she could not go forward either, for she was not brave enough to be eaten by the shark. All she could do was to stay very still and small, and shut her eyes and think with all her strength of the Mother of the Sea, who surely knew she waited at the gates to the palace, holding the sea-child in her arms. And, to comfort herself, Molly began to sing: the sweetest song she had ever heard, that seemed to come from long ago and far away where the stars were born.

Then the shark fell back, his body dissolving in the foam of the waves, and there sat the Mother of the Sea smiling at them from a throne of golden sea-grass. She lifted Molly and the sea-child and they snuggled into the golden folds of her lap. She fed them nectar from the buds of sea lilies, and crisps of purple seaweed. And then she sang to them.

> I sing of the tides and waves of the sea
> From the depths of the ocean where mysteries lie
> Guarded, untouched, unseen and unknown.
> The wild waves surge and the foam licks the sand
> Where the sea meets the moon at the edge of the land.
>
> And the people they laugh and they rage and they cry,
> They fight, they make friends, they live and they die
> My song is of change of the earth and the sea.
> From coco palm beaches to glaciers cold
> I sing of sea changes
> The new and the old.

Then the Mother of the Sea held up a golden pearl and Molly gazed into it and saw her own mother and father and grandmother. They were standing in the lamplight of her parents' bedroom, looking down at a tiny boy.

Immediately, Molly knew that it was her brother, born too early, and she longed to be home to meet him. She was afraid too that, now he was born, she would no longer be loved in the old way.

"Let me go now," she cried, slithering down. "I must go home quickly." The water felt too cold, too salt, too strange. She longed for the softness of dry sand, the warm wooden floor of her room, the cool cotton sheets against her skin.

"I am a child of the land, not the sea." And she was afraid for the first time since she had run from the beach into the moonlit waves.

So the Mother of the Sea kissed her and let her go. Then seals carried her under dark crags, through caverns sounding with the boom of the ocean, through racing waves, back to her room in the house on the beach.

The morning sun shone through the window. With the sea pearl in her pocket, Molly ran downstairs to her parents' room.

"Molly," her mother said, "come and see your brother."

Molly clambered on to the bed and gazed down at the sleeping baby. She saw his tiny hands curled round in a fist. She saw his little red face, screwed up in sleep. Then she held out the sea pearl to him. He opened his eyes and stared up at her, and she smiled with happiness, for she recognised his face. He was the sea-child and she knew they belonged together. She had carried him home.

THE WHISPER

Sheila Powell

Sandy was a new boy, tall and fair, with startling blue eyes and pale skin. He wasn't like the other boys in the school. They were stocky and tough, with dark shock hair and footballers' legs.

Sandy returned their curious looks with a smile. He soon showed them he was willing to play football and could run like the wind.

One day, their teacher, Mrs Pringle, was talking about the tsunami that had struck on the other side of the world. The conversation had moved on to volcanoes – and violent hurricanes with friendly names like Mitch and Charlie. Then she asked them to write their thoughts on any of the things they had been talking about.

This is what Sandy wrote.

In a frozen corner of the earth, where chunks of ice were breaking away and sliding into the sea, the Whisper was born. From the mouth of the Great North Wind, it was released like a sigh and would have slipped into the sea had the Wind not lifted it and sent it on its way.

At the top of their frozen world, the snow bears heard it. Thalar, their king, left his palace of ice and climbed the highest glacier, lifting his white head to listen.

"The elves are coming.

The elves are coming."

The Whisper flew on the icy wind and drew frosty patterns in the air all around him. The snow bear king roared to the world beneath his feet. Then he slipped into the Arctic Waters, carrying the Whisper on his back.

In a blue valley beneath the sea, the whales and dolphins heard it. They swam to the surface and Balee, their king, heaved his great glistening body into the air and crashed back into the waves. Then he drew wide circles in the blue waters and called to his brothers.

The Whisper moved on with the silver shoals across the vast ocean floor and was cast up at last on a bar of golden sand.

"The elves are coming.

The elves are coming."

In the last peaceful jungle of the world, a small herd of elephants stood quietly and listened. They looked up as the Whisper burst apart. Words, like petals, showered down on them. A warm breeze gathered them together and carried the Whisper from tree to tree. Bosca, their great, grey leader, swung his trunk from side to side. Then he lifted it high in the air and bellowed.

The creatures of the jungle heard it and stopped to listen as the Whisper echoed through the air around them. Then the Wind lifted it and carried it to other shores and corners of the world.

On a mountain-top, high above a green valley, a lone eagle heard it. Aquila, queen of the eagles, caught the Wind as it raced past her rocky shelf. With the Whisper on her wings, she swooped down the valley to the forest below. As she flew, she passed on the word to her brothers and sisters.

In the treetops, the Whisper grew into a song and lifted into the air on a thousand voices. High on the back of a cloud, it floated down the valley towards the town.

Above the town the song went on.

No one heard it.

The people were too busy.

Their machines were too noisy.

Their phones were too loud.

The song became a Whisper again.

"Soon", thought the Spirit of the Earth, from whose lips the Whisper had arisen, "soon, the people will be still. Their machines will be quiet. Then they will listen and be glad".

But even when they were still, the people clung to the ground like ants. Not once did they look up or open their hearts to listen.

And their monstrous machines roared on into the night.

At dawn, rain fell upon the grey town.

The Whisper tapped softly on rooftops and windows.

Still, no one heard.

In a field at the edge of the town was a boy. He was searching for mushrooms, humming softly to himself. Suddenly, his tune became a song as words fell upon him with the softly falling rain.

"The elves are coming.

The elves are coming."

The song filled his head and trembled in the air around him. He began to dance the steps of an ancient dance, a dance he had never been taught. Then he stopped and looked at the grey, smoky town, spreading like a stain, swallowing fields and trees.

The sadness inside him was like a stone. He pictured the people scurrying about like moles through tunnels, heads down, always on the move. Machines woke them, fed them. Machines transported them. Machines entertained them. Machines were their servants, their masters. They grew more like them every day.

They had forgotten the old stories, the ways of magic and miracles. They had shut them out with their walls of concrete and steel.

The boy knew what he must do.

He ran back to the town. Surely, the people would be glad when he told them the news. For the elves had disappeared long ago. They had taken with them all the wisdom and knowledge that was Earth's gift to man.

"Listen!" he called to the people as he passed. "The elves are coming! The elves are coming!"

But the people only looked at their watches and hurried past. They thought he was mad, singing in the streets, smiling at everyone.

"Go home, boy!" they said. "Find something useful to do." And on they rushed to their offices and shops and factories.

The boy walked sadly back to the edge of the town and climbed Witch-Wither Hill. He wasn't aware of the footsteps that followed. The children of the town had better hearing than their parents. They had woken from a single dream and felt something good in the air. They had listened and heard the Whisper.

Now the song was beneath his feet, trembling through his toes, rippling over him like warm, summer waves. Louder and louder it grew, until the music drummed all around him like a marching song.

"The elves are coming.

The elves are coming."

Beneath his feet, the heart of Witch-Wither Hill began to beat as up, up they came in their thousands.

From the roots of trees.

From rabbit warrens and molehills.

From fox-earths and badger setts.

And out of the air.

Their long, pale faces shone like stars; their limbs were shafts of light.

The boy sprawled like a cat on the hill, afraid to breathe lest they disappeared. And still they came, carrying books and brooms, spades and hoes, saplings and seeds.

They turned north and south and west, towards rivers and mountains and seas. Not one of them went east towards the town.

"The elves are coming.

The elves are coming."

Now the air was alive with music. Thousands of slender feet tapped out the rhythm, their reed-thin voices singing, humming and whistling as they went.

With each step they stooped gracefully, planting a columbine here, a cowslip there, sprinkling seeds where a hedgerow had been.

Their sigh was as deep as a winter wind when they saw the stump of a felled oak tree. By its side they planted an acorn.

Where they had walked, flowers sprang and shone like stars, and the acorn sent up a pale shoot.

Now, Witch-Wither Hill was covered with children. They joined hands in a circle, crowning the hill, laughing and dancing and singing.

"The elves are here!

The elves are here!"

In the town, the machines roared louder than ever. But the voices of the children lifted into the air and hammered on the walls of concrete and steel.

They would not be silenced.

At last, the people stopped to listen.

They pushed buttons, turned handles, pulled levers, and every machine in the town shuddered, hissed and ground to a halt.

Clocks stopped ticking, phones stopped ringing, motor cars were still, radios were silent.

When all was quiet, the heartbeat of the earth could be heard. The people straightened their backs and lifted their heads to the sky.

The Whisper

Above the grey rooftops and chimneys, a rainbow hung. And the blue sky was full of birds – finches and orioles, lapwings and doves.

The people rubbed their eyes and smiled to see them. They had forgotten how beautiful they were. They heard the children laughing and singing. They walked to the edge of the town and saw forgotten flowers blooming on Witch-Wither Hill. And when they saw the elves, a seed of joy burst inside them, like the memory of a wonderful dream.

Now the children were leaving the hill. They turned north and south and west, their feet treading in the footsteps of the elves. And the people followed, laughing, singing, lifting their faces to the sun.

The Whisper returned to the mouth of the Great North Wind. But the song of the Spirit of the Earth lived on in the hearts of the people – and the Light returned to our World.

Sandy had noticed neither the bell ringing nor the children leaving the classroom, and Mrs Pringle hadn't the heart to disturb his concentration. She sat quietly and waited at her desk. At last, Sandy put down his pen and stood up. He held his book on the palms of his hands like an offering and walked slowly towards her. Mrs Pringle blinked. Had she been dozing for a moment? Was that music playing softly somewhere – and could she hear children's voices chanting, singing? At lunchtime?

She looked at the boy standing with his arms outstretched and it seemed to her that his face shone like the stars and his limbs were shafts of light.

ANN GOES TO WAR

D. K. Jones

Ann sprawled in her seat and stared moodily out of the window of the coach, as the flat, uninteresting French countryside slipped quickly past. Just fourteen years old and the only teenager in a party of middle-aged and elderly people; this wasn't her idea of a holiday! She was bored by the visits to the War cemeteries, with their row upon row of little white crosses, and bored, almost to tears, by the reminiscing of the "old soldiers" in the party. They talked as though they had all stormed their own Normandy beach single-handed in 1944; or was it 1945?

The "Tour of the Battlefields of Europe" had been Dad's idea. He had brought the travel brochures home one evening and said that he had put a deposit on a seven day coach holiday. Mum hadn't been at all pleased. She would have preferred a week in Torquay or some other seaside resort, and said, "It's 1965 and the War has been over for nearly twenty years, so what's the point in spending all that time looking at old battlefields? Everything will have changed."

But she had finally given in when Dad said, "It won't have changed, love. Not for the ones who didn't come home." He'd looked down deep into his cup of tea. "Perhaps I need to go back. I'd like you two with me." Then he'd looked up and smiled. "Just think of it, a luxury coach! We'll be able to sit back and take it easy for seven lazy, carefree days; a bit different from my last trip to France, during the War!"

The boring old War! Weren't the adults ever going to forget it? Ann stretched her arms and legs and yawned.

Well, at least she had a double seat all to herself and didn't have to make polite conversation with anyone, although her mother and father did take it in turns to sit with her occasionally. In another four years she would be eighteen and able to please herself where she went. Four years! Could she put up with these family holidays for that long? She picked up her novel from the empty seat next to her and continued reading. Thank goodness she'd had the foresight to bring several with her!

There was a clicking sound, as the courier picked up his microphone and tested it before speaking. "Well, folks, we are just approaching the motorway café. Time for a short break to stretch your legs! Then we'll be stopping for lunch at about one o'clock. Will you please be back in your seats by eleven o'clock? Thank you."

The coach turned off the motorway and pulled up in a car park at the side of a small motorway café. The passengers noisily disembarked and made their way in small groups towards the entrance. Once inside, they lined up at the food counter. Ann needed to get away from all these people.

"Dad, I think I'll just get a bottle of pop and a packet of crisps from the kiosk and sit outside. It's so stuffy in here."

"Right, dear, but don't wander off; we've only got just over half an hour."

Ann's mother took some coins out of her purse. "You'd better take these, dear. It's more than enough for what you want. And don't forget, we leave at eleven o'clock."

"Thanks, Mum." Ann took the money and bought herself a small bottle of lemonade and a packet of crisps, then strolled out into the warm air.

The ground was still wet from a recent shower, but the sun was shining and she found a wooden bench at the front of the café, near a small copse. The grass underneath the trees seemed to be a strange colour, until Ann noticed that there were hundreds and hundreds of bluebells which covered the ground in a beautiful blue and green carpet.

The bench was still a little wet from the shower so, instead of sitting down, Ann put her lemonade and the packet of crisps on it and walked across to take a closer look at the bluebells. Along the edge of the wood was a shallow ditch and, as Ann reached it, her foot slipped on the wet grass and she stumbled forward, banging her head as she fell and losing consciousness.

Ann got up to find herself lying in the bottom of the ditch, her hands and clothes covered in mud. "Oh, no!" she thought, "I'd better get back to the café and try to clean up a bit before Mum sees me."

She started to scramble out of the ditch, then stopped, puzzled. The bench, with her lemonade and crisps, had vanished. So had the motorway café, and in its place was a small cottage. Ann wondered what was happening. Was she dreaming? She remembered that, in situations like this, people were supposed to pinch themselves, so she nipped the back of her left hand. "Ow! Well, I'm not dead, anyway!" The sound of her own voice reassured her. Could she have knocked herself out when she fell? Was this a dream? That must be it!

She looked over the top of the ditch towards the cottage and saw three men crouching behind some small bushes near the front porch. They would be able to direct her back to the café. But there was something strange about them. Ann looked again and saw that they were wearing helmets and greyish uniforms. She'd seen pictures like that in War films her father watched on television; they were German soldiers! Still hidden by the tall grass on the edge of the ditch, Ann stared open-mouthed at the soldiers, then saw that one of them was crouching over a machine-gun.

At that moment, some men carrying rifles emerged from the trees on the far side of the cottage. Still trying to collect her senses, Ann gasped as she recognised them as British soldiers. There were about twenty of them, and they walked steadily towards the front of the cottage, obviously not aware of the hidden Germans.

Ann watched, horrified, as the advancing men reached the side of the cottage. Just a few more paces, and those in front would be in line with the machine gun. Without thinking of the danger to herself, she stood up, pointed towards the crouching Germans, and shouted at the top of her voice, "Germans! Germans!" Then, realising what she had done, she jumped backwards into the muddy ditch.

For what seemed ages, the sound of gunfire filled the air. Then there were two loud explosions. Ann felt sick and started shivering. She crouched even further down in the ditch. After the explosions, there was the sound of raised voices, then complete silence. Even the birds had stopped singing. The silence was broken by the sound of footsteps. Ann shuddered. Someone was approaching her hiding place. Was one of the Germans coming to shoot her?

The footsteps stopped, and Ann looked up to see a young British Army sergeant peering down at her, a revolver in his hand. He looked up and down the ditch, then put the gun back in its holster.

"Well, muddy little French girl, do you speak English?" Still shaking, all Ann could do was nod.

"Good. Thank you very much for saving our lives. If it hadn't been for you, those Jerries would have made mincemeat of us."

The sergeant pointed toward the cottage, where the three Germans were standing with their hands raised above their heads, near the overturned machine gun. Ann stared wide-eyed at the sergeant, still unable to speak.

"You look very shaken. Here, would you like a little swig of brandy?" The sergeant took a small bottle from his pocket and held it down towards her. "Sorry. I haven't anything else." Ann continued to stare at him, still unable to find her voice. She shook her head.

"No, that was silly of me. No brandy for little girls! I suppose the couple in the cottage are your parents? They are quite safe, so you'll be all right. Now I've got to take the prisoners in, but here ...." The sergeant took a small cross on a gold chain from around his neck, knelt on the edge of the ditch, reached down, and put it in the pocket of Ann's blouse.

"You saved my life, brave little French girl. I want you to have this, to say 'Thank you' for your very courageous deed. That cross is very special to me. My grandmother gave it to me when I joined the Army, to bring me luck. Well, today you were that luck."

Ann struggled to get out of the ditch, but the sergeant gestured for her to stay where she was. "No, stay in hiding for a while. The shooting might have attracted more Jerries. They might try to free my prisoners. But I'll let your parents know where you are, and they can come and fetch you when we've gone." The sergeant leaned forward and kissed Ann's muddy forehead, then got up and walked towards the cottage.

Still unable to speak, Ann just stared after him. He'd called her a "little French girl", and whoever the people in the cottage were, they certainly were not her parents! Anxious to find out what was happening to her, she started to clamber out of the ditch, but slipped and fell back in, bumping her head. "Not again!" she whispered, as everything became enveloped in a soft, white mist.

Ann opened her eyes and saw her father bending over her. She was lying on the grass not far from the bench, on which stood her small bottle of lemonade and the packet of crisps.

"How do you feel, dear?"

"I don't know, Dad." Ann tried to sit up. "I've got a sore head."

Her mother knelt down and tried to wipe some of the mud off Ann's face with a handkerchief. "You must have fallen into the ditch and bumped your head, dear. We've been looking for you everywhere."

Her father said, "Well, Annie girl, I've done some First Aid in my time, some of it near this very place, come to think of it! There don't appear to be any bones broken; just a couple of nasty bumps on your head. Can you get up?"

As he helped her to her feet, Ann was surprised to find that she wasn't even giddy. "I'm fine now, Dad, apart from a headache." She looked towards the motorway café. No cottage, no soldiers. It must have been a dream; or rather, a nightmare, brought on by the first bump on the head.

The coach driver pushed his way through the group of onlookers. "The facilities in the café aren't very good, but there's a hotel about two miles down the road. If you like, we can stop there and your daughter can have a hot bath and a change of clothes."

On the way back to the coach, Ann looked up at her mother. "Mum, I had this dream."

"Yes, dear. It won't be long now before we get to the hotel."

Why wouldn't her parents listen properly? This was so important. "Dad!"

"Bumps on the head sometimes have that effect, Annie girl. You'll feel a lot better after a bath and change of clothes."

Soon the coach was once again speeding along the motorway. Ann's father was sitting beside her. "Still feel all right, apart from the bumps on the head?"

"Fine. Dad, that dream ..."

Her father leaned across and looked out of the window. "It seems hard to believe that, only about twenty years ago, this was a battlefield. The bombed houses have all disappeared. The trenches and shell holes, all gone. Just like after the First World War."

"My dream, Dad ..."

Her father continued to look out of the window. "Funny how places change. My mob came right across this part of France just after D-Day."

Ann tugged her father's arm. "Dad, my dream! I saw soldiers, British soldiers and Germans too. It was so horrible. The soldiers were so young, Dad!" She looked around the coach, realising for the first time that her nightmare had been reality for all these men. "I'll never grumble again when I hear people talking about the War."

Her father looked surprised and smiled at her. "That must have been some dream, Ann. Yes, we were young. Look!" He took his wallet out of his pocket and extracted a dog-eared photograph. "Here, look at me before I grew my moustache! I was just eight years older than you are now."

Ann felt as if her heart was leaping out of her chest. She stared, unbelievingly, at the picture of a young, clean-shaven, British Army sergeant. She gulped, then whispered. "I think I'll have that brandy now, Dad."

"Brandy? What do you mean?" Her father stared at her in amazement.

Ann put her hand in her blouse pocket and gasped with surprise as she felt the chain with the cross attached.

"Dad!" Ann took the cross and chain out of her pocket. "Remember this, Dad? Your grandmother gave it to you, to bring you luck."

Her father was momentarily speechless as he stared unbelievingly at the cross and chain. He spoke very quietly, "But Annie, but I gave it to ..."

Ann interrupted him, "Me, dad. You gave it to me."

WHEN THE GIRAFFE CAME TO OUR HOUSE

David Diggory

Once, years ago, when sitting in my bedroom reading a book, I looked up to see a face, staring at me through the window. It was not a human face. It had big eyes with curly eyelashes, and a long, narrow head with nibbly lips. Furthermore, it was yellow, with large, brown spots. I put my book on the bed, and shouted downstairs: "Mum! There's a giraffe in the front garden!"

And so there was.

Mum, Dad and I stood outside and looked at the giraffe, and pondered what to do. "We could call the RSPCA," said Dad.

"But "RSPCA" stands for "Royal Society for the Prevention of *Cruelty* to Animals," said Mum. "And nobody is being cruel to him."

"We could telephone the local zoo," I said, "and see if they can take him."

"We can't do that," said Mum. "They are always short of money, and couldn't possibly cope with another mouth to feed."

We pondered again and, at length, Mum said, "We could invite him in for tea."

And so we did. And the giraffe seemed to smile as he followed us inside.

Now, it wasn't easy, having a giraffe in the house. He couldn't sit in the living room, for the sofa was too small, and he couldn't sit in the kitchen, for Mum kept tripping over his hooves, while she set the tray. In the end, he parked himself in the hallway, his bottom wedged between the telephone table and the wall, his neck stretching up the stairs, his head resting neatly on the landing, where we all sat, with tea and scones, and kept pleasant company.

I suppose you might be thinking our giraffe finished sipping his tea from Mum and Dad's best china service and, with a polite nod of thanks, returned from whence he came. But, you'd be wrong! The giraffe, it seemed, had no intention of going.

"My, it's late!" said Dad, looking at his watch, and hoping the giraffe might take the hint.

"I really must get back to my book," said I, thinking much the same thing.

But Mum took a different view. "Why, the fellow's only just arrived! He can't possibly go, yet."

So, while Dad and I made our way awkwardly downstairs to wash the dishes, Mum sat and talked to the giraffe. Then, while we went into the garden and grumbled it really was inconsiderate of the beast to stay into the evening, Mum patted the giraffe, gently. And after twilight had fallen, and Dad and I had gone inside the house to get warm, Mum crooned the giraffe a lullaby, until he peacefully slept, his head cradled by a large feather pillow.

"Now, don't you wake him!" she ordered, as we edged cautiously past, and made our way to bed.

There are many things you might read about giraffes: that they are capable of outrunning a gazelle; that they can be fierce when protecting their young; that they have the longest necks in the entire animal kingdom. The one fact you will not read is that they snore. The giraffe in our house snored so badly we thought he would blow the roof off.

Dad stood on the landing in his dressing gown and pyjamas and said, "I can't stand it!"

I stood on the landing in my dressing gown and pyjamas and said, "I can't stand it!"

Mum stood on the landing in her dressing gown and nightie and said, "Now you know what *I* have to put up with!" Then she returned to bed, and within minutes was fast asleep.

The next morning, Dad and I, both bleary-eyed, left the house, Dad to work, I to school. I said to my class, "There's a giraffe at our house."

My teacher, Miss Phipps said, "Don't make up silly stories, Howard," and threatened to report me to the headmaster if I persisted.

Dad told his boss, Mr Pottiswood, about the giraffe and he said, "Listen, Rogers, you've been working too hard lately. It's time you took a holiday." Dad agreed he did need a holiday, but he didn't want one offered only because his boss thought he had imagined a giraffe in the house.

Mum was also due to go to work, but she telephoned her boss, Mr Candela, and said, "I'm sorry I can't come in today, because I have a giraffe to look after." Mr Candela replied that if Mum could not think of a more believable excuse, she had better look for another job.

After Mum had made the giraffe breakfast of toast, coffee and orange juice, she stayed with him all day, chatting and playing her guitar. She sang a composition entitled, "The Love I Once Had", which is her favourite, and what adults call a "weepie". She was in floods of tears when Dad and I got home, and had to explain it was because of the song, and not because the giraffe had become a strain.

Eventually, word of the giraffe got out. Miss Phipps apologised for implying I lived in a fantasy world and organised a school trip, especially to see the creature. The school bus pulled up outside our house and everyone cried, "Where is he? Where is he?", until his face appeared spookily in the frosted pane of the toilet window.

"Howard, you're very lucky to have this giraffe staying with you," said Miss Phipps, and I wanted to agree - but there was, of course, that snoring.

Mr Pottiswood called Dad to his office and said, "Fantastic, Hyram! This is a golden opportunity for publicity!" Dad worked in a business importing oranges, and Mr Pottiswood organised TV, radio and the Press to come by. They stood outside, with their vans and their cameras, their notebooks and their pencils, and they filmed Mr Pottiswood grinning by our gate, saying, "Pottiswood's Oranges. Peel a Pottiswood for the giraffe in your family."

Mr Candela got to hear about the giraffe by seeing it on the local TV 'News'. What would everyone say, he thought, if they found he'd not wanted to give Mum time off to look after the giraffe? He called straight away and told her to come back to work when convenient, and not one moment sooner.

You will have gathered not everyone in our family was happy with the situation. I was not happy because it was difficult to concentrate on my homework with the giraffe watching from the landing. Dad was not happy because the giraffe seemed to be getting more attention from Mum than he did. And even Mum found it mildly irritating to reach over the giraffe's bottom every time she wanted to use the telephone.

There were advantages, however. First, I had become very popular at school. I gave a talk, entitled "Giraffes, And How to Entertain Them". I described how Mum made Dad and me perform a sand dance with a tea towel on our heads, to make the guest feel at home – even though Dad expressed doubt over the proximity of giraffes to the Nile and its tributaries. Secondly, Dad received a bonus for increased sales of "Pottiswood's Finest Oranges". And there were occasions, when the giraffe moved to assist us in our daily lives, that we found it useful to have him around: he helped Mum pick the apples from the apple tree; he held the bucket of soapy water when Dad cleaned the windows; and he retrieved my football when it became stuck on the garage roof.

But these advantages were far outweighed ....

"Shut the sunshine roof!" cried Dad, whenever it rained, and the giraffe was a passenger in his car – but Mum wouldn't hear of it.

"Get out of the way!" shouted a patron from the back row of the cinema, when the giraffe insisted on a middle seat.

"You're useless," I complained, when once I persuaded the giraffe to play hide-and-seek – for indeed he was.

So it was not without relief one day, sitting in my bedroom reading a book, that I looked up to see a face, staring at me through the window. It was not a human face. It had big eyes with curly eyelashes, and a long, narrow head with nibbly lips. Furthermore, it was yellow, with large, brown spots. I put my book on the bed, and shouted downstairs: "Mum! There's *another* giraffe in the front garden!"

There came a mighty heaving and shoving as our giraffe decided to investigate this new giraffe for himself and, by the time I reached the landing, he was outside, and by the time Mum, Dad and I stood in the front garden, he and the new giraffe had their necks entwined, and were staring longingly into each other's eyes.

"It seems he has found a companion," said Dad, sounding hopeful. And with that, the two giraffes made their way out of our drive, and down the street – never to be seen again.

And only Mum was sad.

CHOMPING ON A SWEET SONG

Jane Mack

Narrator: As old as an oak,
with hair like smoke,
Granny Smith hob-hobbles along,
her face like a dried-up apple,
her mouth chomping on a sweet song.

As blind as a mole
in a tar-black hole,
Granny Smith hobbles up the steep hill,
hand in hand with eight-year-old Susan:
her grand-child who lives at the mill.

Her eyes shining bright
as a glow-worm's light,
Susan tugs at her Gran's wrinkled hand.
"Susan, what is that smell so orange and
        warm,
like a desert of smiling sand?"

Susan: "That's the baker's, Gran;
it's the baker, Dan.
You know, he's all floating in flour.
He plaited sixty harvest loaves;
it took him less than an hour."

Gran: "I hear a chime
telling the time.
Let's count the sounds of the bell,
each separate and rounded,
sweet as a caramel."

Word Weaving

Both:
"One is for walking,
two is for talking,
three is for threading our way
round the curves of the hill
to Greengrocer Bill.
Tell me, what will he say?"

"Four is for fruit,
five is for flute,
which the greengrocer plays in a band,
six for a sweet satsuma,
like a harvest moon in your hand."

Gran:
"Seven's for sage
and eight is for age:
together we have ninety years.
We share the same strong sunlit dreams,
the same sad, shadowy fears."

Narrator:
They've reached the top,
and the clippety-clop
of hooves fills the air all around.
"Gran, Gran, his long mane
is like windwaves through grain,"
says Susan; then, "Look what I've found!"

She quickly stoops
and nimbly scoops
a stone from the chalky soil.
Her grandmother sees with her bony hands,
as she fingers the fossilised coil.

Gran:
"That was a creature.
It's kept every feature
from when it lived, long, long ago,"

Chomping on a Sweet Song

whispers the woman whose spine is all
        curved
and who, like a snail, is now slow.

Narrator: As old as an oak,
           with hair like smoke,
           Granny Smith hob-hobbles along,
           her face like a dried-up apple,
           her mouth chomping on a sweet song.

THE RELUCTANT CABIN BOY

Vanessa Greatorex

"No! I don't want to be a cabin boy! Put me down!" Tom struggled with all his might, thrashing his legs like eels in a trap, but the iron grip clamping his arms tightened even more.

"Can't do that," said the man in the red scarf, the hoop of his earring glinting in the sunlight. "Cap'n's orders. I'm to bring the first boy I see back on board. So you're coming along o' me, and the sooner you learn to do as Cap'n says, the better it'll be for you."

"Look!" said Tom, casting desperately round and catching sight of a skinny lad throwing stones at the seagulls. "Over there!" He jutted his chin towards the north. "That's Jem Whaley. Why don't you take him instead of me? He loves the sea. It's in his blood. His dad's a master mariner, and he plans to be one too." Tom's struggles ceased as he sought to convince his captor. "He'd do you proud as a cabin boy. I'll be useless. I'm a landlubber through and through."

"Ah, but that's the thing," said a new voice, deeper, dangerous, yet tinged with an echo of the Squire's silken tones. "Excitement. Adventure. Treasure. It's an invigorating life, and I've experienced it to the full."

Tom's darting gaze encountered a man with liquid amber eyes and a nose cruel as a falcon's beak.

"But now I want a new challenge." The red velvet of the Captain's coat scintillated in the four o'-clock sun. He leaned towards Tom, the brim of his black hat almost grazing the boy's fair hair. "Where's the triumph in taking a master mariner's son to sea? I want to turn an unwilling prig of a scaredy-cat into the boldest pirate who ever sailed the seven seas."

"Actually, there are more than seven seas," declaimed Tom before he could stop himself. "So Reverend Hewetson says," he added hastily. The boys of Shotwick hated a clever clogs, and he suspected pirates were no different in that respect.

"Reverend Hewetson, eh?" said the Captain. "I know him of old."

Tom's eyes widened in surprise. His mentor, his guide, the white-haired guardian of parish morals - acquainted with a pirate? How? Why?

But there was no time to ponder the conundrum, for the Captain was still speaking. "Is he your tutor?"

"Yes," said Tom. "He thinks if I work hard enough, I might get a scholarship to Oxford. Then I can become an attorney and earn enough money to free my parents from a lifetime of grubbing in the soil."

"A lawyer?" The Captain's laugh was harsh and brief.

"Dirtier work than farming," spat the pirate in the red scarf. "And you'll spend a mort of money aping the ways of the gentry. It'll help your parents more if you come away with us. One less mouth for 'em to feed and untold riches if we strike lucky."

"Haynes is right," said the Captain. "Bide your time and serve me well, and I'll not see you the loser."

Tom said nothing as Haynes frogmarched him to the *Black Stallion*. But his mind was working furiously. *"Bide my time? Good advice. Just you wait, Captain."*

The wind howled. The darkness swirled. The *Black Stallion* reared and fell in the clasp of the North Sea. The hatches were battened, the sails furled and all hands on deck beneath the pelting sky. Tom had never been so wet, so cold, so utterly uncomfortable. And yet there surged within him a spark of exultation as he stood tense as a bowstring, ready to play his part in delivering the ship from evil.

"There!" he cried. "Nor'-nor'-west. A brig. She's listing."

"She's ours!" said the Captain, straining the *Black Stallion*'s wheel towards his prey.

A drawn sword. A menacing laugh. A manic gleam in the eye. Capturing the crippled brig was as easy as posturing on stage. But Tom found its cargo disappointing.

"Manx kippers?" he said in disgust. "Wool?"

"And brandy besides," gloated Haynes.

"Don't look so crestfallen, lad," said the Captain. "It may not be Spanish gold or rubies, but it's a blow for free trade." He raised his voice. "We head for port!"

Two days later, in the mirk-midnight, when the North Sea storm had blown itself out, Tom watched from the bows of the *Black Stallion* as his shipmates manoeuvred kegs and bales into a lowered boat.

"You may be the fastest learner I've ever met," said the Captain, lashing Tom to the mast, "but I'm not going to trust you on land yet. You'll stay here with Haynes until we've finished our business ashore."

"Aye, aye, Cap'n," said Tom.

The Captain shot a suspicious look at the boy's face, but encountered only bland obedience.

As the weeks slid by and Tom showed no sign of defying the Captain, he became a trusted member of the *Black Stallion*'s crew. His sharp eyes were always the first to spot a ship on the horizon. He was agile on the rigging and deft with a needle. He took no part in hand-to-hand fighting, but his conscience seemed untroubled when it was time to stow stolen goods in the hold or engage in a spot of smuggling. He sang with the crew on balmy summer nights, and worked with a will when the weather changed its tune.

And all the time he wondered. Why did the Captain sing hymns when he boarded a captive ship, sword drawn and mercy forgotten? What had made him choose a cabin boy from Shotwick, when he could have had any lad from any coastal town in Britain? And where had Tom seen those amber eyes before?

Then, one evening, as they stacked French brandy in the cellar of a Devonshire parson, the facts clicked into place.

"You remind me of someone I knew years ago," said the parson, eyeing the Captain's velvet coat with envy. "A fellow student of Divinity. I must find out where he has his living. He might welcome your services."

"That would be most kind," said the Captain with a bow. "New customers are always welcome."

On the way back to the *Black Stallion*, Tom was struck by an image of a very different parson: his tutor, the Reverend Hewetson, opposed to smuggling, a vociferous critic of pirates, yet apparently acquainted with the Captain. Parsons - smuggling - hymns - amber eyes. In a flash, Tom realised the new customer would never materialise. But the moment for acknowledging his insight had not arrived.

The months galloped forward in a whirl of piracy, and Tom's jerkin grew steadily heavier as he sewed his share of stolen gold into its lining. Then, one day, a hornpipe of butterflies tickled his stomach as the tidal waters of the Dee bore the *Black Stallion* up the Wirral shoreline. It was a year to the day since he'd last seen home, and time to confront the Captain.

"I know who you are," he said. "And why you wanted a boy from Shotwick."

"Do you indeed?" said the Captain. "Pray, enlighten the crew."

"You're the Squire's long-lost uncle." Tom looked the Captain straight in his tell-tale amber eyes. "The one who became a country parson, then disappeared without a trace."

The Captain quirked an eyebrow. "And why would such a pillar of the community want to become a pirate?"

"Boredom," said Tom. "You craved excitement and adventure. You'd always loathed village life. But you never forgot your priestly training. And having engineered your own lucky escape, you thought you'd give thanks to God by bestowing a similar favour on some poor oaf from your native village."

"How kind of me," said the Captain.

"The thing is, this is *my* life," said Tom. "Mine. I want to follow my own path, not the one someone else has chosen for me. And, thanks to the gold I earned as your cabin boy, I can now afford to do exactly that. I want comfort. I want an education. I want freedom - and I'm claiming it now."

Grasping a rope dangling from the rigging, Tom swung forward and planted his feet squarely on the Captain's chest. As the Captain staggered backwards, Tom leapt on to the rim of the ship, bowed to his shipmates, and executed a perfect dive into the water.

Haynes crossed the deck in a couple of strides, intent on diving after Tom.

"Let him go," said the Captain. "I taught him well. That's no cabin boy. That's a man who knows what he wants and bides his time till he gets it. A man who leaves without a pang. A man who fears no one and nothing, not even me. That, Haynes, is the boldest pirate who ever sailed the seven seas." The Captain straightened his back and placed his hat more firmly on his head. "I have risen to my challenge. This calls for rum!"

And the crew raised their tots to the receding back of Tom the scholar, Tom the pirate, Tom the attorney and gentleman.

THURSDAY AFTERNOON SHOWDOWN

Gary Hayden

Thursday afternoon. Five past three. Ten minutes 'til going-home time.

The second hand crawled around the clock face. A large bluebottle bumped repeatedly against the classroom window. *Sorry, mate,* I muttered beneath my breath. *You're stuck in here with the rest of us.*

Mr McWroe continued to drone on about life in Victorian England. I'd stopped listening ages ago.

My mind drifted back to the film I'd watched on telly the previous night. One of those old black and white ones they show on Channel 4: *Lonesome Gunslinger.*

What a great film - cowboys really led an exciting life - the final showdown was brilliant - I'd love to be a gunslinger - bet I'd be quick on the draw - and a real cool cowboy.

In my imagination, I was standing in the main street of a small American town, back in the 1800s. The jaunty sound of a honky-tonk piano filtered out from a nearby saloon; the sheriff chewed tobacco on the porch outside the jailhouse; and saloon girls in brightly-coloured underwear giggled together on a hotel balcony.

I just stood there. Right in the middle of the street. Waiting.

Three horses galloped into town. Their riders certainly believed in making an entrance. They laughed, yeeee-hawed and fired guns into the air as they rode. Then, with a sharp tug on the reins, they brought the horses to a stop, raising a cloud of dust.

The honky-tonk piano trailed off into silence; the sheriff spat out his tobacco and hightailed it into the safety of the jailhouse; and the saloon girls ran shrieking into their hotel room.

Within seconds the street had emptied, leaving just the three riders and me.

The biggest, meanest-looking rider dismounted. He took a cigar from his lips, threw it down, and ground it into the dust.

"So," he said, pausing to blow out a last mouthful of cigar smoke. "You're the no-good son-of-a-sidewinder who shot my brother?"

"Your brother had it coming," I replied, voice icy-cool.

"Well, now *you* got it comin'," he snarled, pulling open his overcoat to reveal a brown leather holster and a Colt-45 pistol.

I narrowed my eyes, placed my hands at the ready over my double holster, and waited for him to make the first move....

Mr McWroe's voice interrupted my thoughts. "Richard Green – I asked you a question!"

"Sorry?"

He sighed. The heavy sigh of a teacher who's sick and tired of speaking to kids who can't be bothered listening. "I asked you a question, lad. Do you think that life for Victorian children was better or worse than it is for children today?"

I shook myself awake, and put on my best "thinking-hard-about-the-question-but-not-really-managing-to-come-up-with-a-suitable-answer" face.

At that point, Mr McWroe ought to have done the decent thing. He'd shaken me out of my daydream, got my attention and embarrassed me a bit. Fair enough. But then he ought to have let the matter drop - asked somebody else.

But he didn't. He focused his gaze more closely upon me, and raised his eyebrows as if to say, *I'm waiting.*

He wanted to make me squirm – to demonstrate my ignorance to the entire class.

I carried on pulling my "thinking-hard-about-the-question" face, but said nothing. Mr McWroe leaned forward across his desk and looked me squarely in the eye.

The silence was becoming uncomfortable. I could have broken the tension simply by saying something. Almost anything would have done. I could have apologised for not listening, or said that life was worse for Victorian kids because they didn't have DVDs and chicken nuggets. Then he'd have made a sarcastic comment and left me alone.

But something hardened inside me. I somehow just didn't feel like doing things his way. So I decided to make a stand – to square-up against him in a battle of will and nerve.

I looked back at him and said nothing.

I glanced at the classroom clock out of the corner of my eye. It was ten past three. Five minutes 'til the bell.

And so began the Thursday Afternoon Showdown. Mr McWroe and me. Face to face. Man-to-man. Cowboys without cows. Gunslingers without guns.

Tick .. tick .. tick.

The classroom clock counted away the long seconds.

Mr McWroe continued to look at me, eyebrows raised, waiting for a response. I continued to pull my "thinking-hard" face, and remained silent.

A minute passed, and the silence deepened. You could actually *feel* it.

Tick .. tick .. tick.

Mr McWroe leaned further over his desk. The eyes of the class flitted back and forth between us. A girl on the back row let out a nervous giggle, which she quickly stifled. Other kids fiddled uneasily with pens and rulers.

Tick .. tick .. tick .

Another minute passed - much slower than the one before. Three minutes until the bell.

Mr McWroe placed the palms of his hands together, fingers outstretched, fingertips touching. His gaze took on an air of menace. I dropped my "thinking-hard" expression, and merely looked back at him. Not cheeky. Not rebellious. But not frightened either. I just *looked* at him.

Tick .. tick .. tick .

Another minute passed - the longest of my entire life. Two minutes left until the bell. Two agonising minutes.

Who would crack first? Would the pressure get to me, so that I started apologising, or garbling on about Victorian England? Or would he be first to succumb, by making some sarcastic comment, or passing the question to someone else?

Tick .. tick .. tick.

The silence had become almost unbearable. A tiny bead of perspiration appeared on Mr McWroe's forehead. I found myself holding my breath. Even the bluebottle stopped its buzzing, and stood motionless on the windowsill.

Tick .. tick .. tick.

Another minute passed. One more to go.

Mr McWroe stood up. He didn't utter a word, but he eyed me with undisguised venom – with a look that said, *Answer the question or I'll make your life a living hell.*

My heart hammered inside my chest, and I could hear my blood rushing through my ears. But I'd come too far to back down. It was death or glory.

I just had to hold my nerve a few seconds longer....

Tick .. tick .. tick .. *brrrrinnng!*

47

The going-home time bell rang, and the class let out a collective sigh of relief. Springing up from the windowsill, the bluebottle resumed its buzzing and bumping. The other kids gathered their belongings and made a hasty escape.

Within seconds the classroom had emptied, leaving just Mr McWroe and me.

"So," he said, icily "You really have nothing to say about the lives of children in Victorian England?"

"Afraid not, Sir."

"Then perhaps you ought to do some research at the library, and write me a two-page essay - by tomorrow morning."

"Yes, Sir."

I walked out through the classroom door, closed it behind me, and swaggered out into the corridor. I felt great. True, I had a two-page essay to write. But *he'd* spoken first.

I'd emerged victorious from the Thursday Afternoon Showdown.

WHEN STONES SHED TEARS

I. E. Challender

Kizzie was fizzing with excitement, like a firework about to explode. She had waited so long for the day of the wedding, counting the months, then the days, but now she had only hours to wait until tomorrow. Her long bridesmaid's dress was beautiful – an unusual colour her mother described as "claret"; adding in the hard, dismissive tone she often reserved for Kizzie:

"Perhaps a little mature for her, but it does help light up that pale skin and hair."

Truly, Kizzie's hair was glorious – a golden sunburst of curly fronds – but as difficult to discipline as Kizzie herself. The sight of a brush and comb meant a declaration of war, and led to frequent battles with her Mum. However, now a truce had been declared. Kizzie's hair was to be professionally styled and crowned with a wreath to go to church.

Unfortunately, Kizzie had a problem, and it concerned the church. Not the high dim arches of the roof where she imagined spiders were hunting and weaving gossamer webs in the darkness. Not the soft diffused light from the windows that glowed like jewels when the sun shone through. What disturbed Kizzie was the tomb chests, where the stone effigies of knights and their ladies still slept as they had for centuries, but with a sense of quiet awareness and anticipation as if they hovered on the brink of awakening. She was especially troubled by the tomb of the boy prince who, according to her history teacher, had been killed during the Wars of the Roses. His stone effigy was intact, not mutilated like some of the others, and the coronet he wore was brightly gilded, drawing the sun to

49

light his creamy marble face. In her mind, Kizzie could see him in every perfect detail, and also the crystal teardrop that had rested in the corner of his closed eye. Where had it come from - that drop of moisture? There was no leaking window, no rain dripping from the roof. It was definitely a tear. To prove it to herself, she had touched it gently with her fingertip and tasted it. It was as salty as her own tears, shed in the latest stormy duel with her mother. But the prince was a warrior. Why would he shed tears?

Turning over the problem, she realised that now, while everyone was busy, she had the opportunity to sneak out of the house and go to the church for another look at the prince. The evening glowed warm with the heat of the day as she raced through the churchyard, hoping to find the church door unlocked, but it was strangely heavy and she struggled to push it open. The intense cold inside hit her like a blow and, shivering, she searched the gloom for the prince. In the fading light, the effigy looked very lifelike and somehow not so peaceful; tortured, in fact, as if trying to free itself from the stone. Kizzie lost her courage and turned to leave, when she heard her name. It was the voice of a boy, breaking into manhood, husky, the pitch uncertain, but the command unmistakable:

"Stay - if you please". The prince had raised himself on one elbow and had turned his head to look her full in the face, while his arm was stretched out to her. "We're linked, you and I. You tasted my tears and I have tasted yours when you have come here, distraught and weeping."

Kizzie was totally "gobsmacked", but her self-possession returned and she found voice enough to explain, "Oh, that was my Mum. She gets me down sometimes. But why were you crying?"

The prince's form was becoming less substantially marble, she noticed, and more flesh-like, with delicately coloured tones in skin, hair and eyes. His robe had softened into fabric that was the colour of her bridesmaid's dress, yet there was no solidity about him. It seemed that, if she tried to touch him, her hand might go straight through, so she decided not to try and concentrated instead on what he was saying.

"How can I help weeping, when I consider what I lost through one impetuous action? My destiny was to become king. I was my father's only heir, and with my death he lost his throne and his own life, when his enemies exacted a terrible revenge. Oh, but Kizzie – I dreamed of winning glory on the battlefield like my ancestors. Because I was considered grown to manhood, I had new armour and my destrier was a big, spirited, black stallion, armed, plumed, and trained to rear and fight with teeth and flailing hooves. He was excited and restless, but I had him well under control. My sword was a wonderfully balanced weapon, honed to perfection by the armourers and, as I'd been practising the use of arms since the age of seven, I was confident that I would acquit myself well in this, my first battle.

"As if it were the joust, I sat on the hilltop in splendour among bright flags and waving pennants, surrounded by the lords of my retinue, while the first clash of arms took place in the field below. The fighting raged, arrows flew, and still we sat until, seething with impatience, I dug my spurs into my horse's flanks and sent him into the thick of the fight – poor beast – straight on to the point of a lance through his belly. Pinned down by his fall, surrounded by screaming, hacking, bloodstained men, I cried then in terror for my nurse, a friend, my companions-in-arms, someone, but I was totally alone when they turned their weapons upon me. There was no quarter for a royal prince. My head, with the coronet on it, was too great a prize. Many others found no glory that day – just the same sordid, bloody death – and for them I will weep eternally.

"Above all, after these many years, I suppose I weep for the loneliness that is so hard to bear. My marriage had been arranged to a princess of France, whose likeness resembled yours, with the same golden curling hair. She would have shared my life, and in death her effigy would have lain beside mine. Yet I never had the chance to meet or know her, whereas I have watched you, Kizzie, and our tears have mingled. If you take my hand now and come to me, you and I would never know loneliness and heartbreak again. You would be my princess forever and I your prince to command, your hair crowned with a golden coronet, not just a bridesmaid's wreath."

He stretched his hand towards Kizzie and she felt compelled to move towards him – her hand rising, her arm trembling as it extended towards his, their fingers now almost touching.

"Kizzie", he pleaded, but his voice faded as she hesitated.

"Kizzie" - a different voice surely; the same pleading tone, but a different voice. "Kizzie, honey. Oh, do come back to me. My God, what can I do? There's so much blood, and she's so pale and cold. Why doesn't she speak to me?"

Kizzie realised it was her mother's voice, sounding, not coldly irritated, but unusually tender, while the hand she had stretched out to the prince was now imprisoned and gently pressed to her mother's lips, wet with her mother's tears. Kizzie became aware she was hurting in so many different places and her eyes just wouldn't open. It was just too much trouble to talk. A pity – she would have liked to ask the prince if this was how he felt after the battle, but there was a man's voice now, calm and reassuring.

"She'll be fine. Scalp injuries look bad because they bleed profusely, but that thick mop of hair helped to minimise the damage. We're going to move her now, but you can ride with her to the hospital. We nearly had to take Vicar too. It gave him quite a shock to have your lass charge out of the bushes headlong into the side of his car like that. He thought there was someone with her, but if so, they didn't hang around after the accident to help. Isn't Vicar officiating at the wedding tomorrow? It's a shame, but this bridesmaid will miss her day in church, I'm afraid."

Strangely, the lusty, protesting wail which burst from Kizzie's lips encouraged her mother and the small band of onlookers who had been drawn to the scene by the siren and the flashing blue lights of the ambulance. Vicar's car had swerved off the track and reared up against an ancient tomb in the graveyard, displaying the dent in its side like a wound. Vicar himself – unhorsed, so to speak – sat shakily on a lichen-covered stone slab. Was it his voice Kizzie heard now, or another, so close it could have been inside her head? Was it the quavering voice of an old man or a distraught boy that exclaimed, "Ah, Kizzie - so you've chosen to live and fight another day."

OCCHI AND THE RAINBOW

Juliet Watkinson

This story is dedicated with lasting respect and affection
to
Sue Welshman

~o~O~o~

What has blue blood?
Blue blood and nine brains?
An alien?

No.
Try again.

~o~O~o~

What has a body like a bag of wobbly jelly?

What has ~
not one arm,
not two arms,
not three arms,
not four arms,
not five arms,
not six arms
not *even* seven arms ~

but

Eight Arms and **No Fingers ?**

54

Occhi and the Rainbow

Occhi is an octopus who lives in a secret place under the sea.

He is very proud of his home. No one has ever seen it, because it is such a very secret and private place. It suits Occhi perfectly. There is just enough room for his wobbly body and his eight long arms.

When he wakes up, he puts his eight arms outside and waves them about in the sea currents.

When he wants to sleep, he carefully brings each arm in, one by one.

He feels very snug and safe and sound when all his arms are safely inside.

He really should have been a very happy octopus.

But Occhi did not like the colour of his wobbly body and his eight arms. They were a colour we have no name for: a murky grey-green-blue colour ~ a wobbly-wet colour ~ a seaweedy, rocky, water-jelly kind of colour.

This peculiar wobbly colour was a good colour to be, because Occhi matched his home exactly. If you swam past his home you would never be able to see him ~ even if he had his arms out and was waving at you! Tangerine tetras, blue barracudas, pink prawns and silver sprats just swam by without seeing him. Even the crimson crabs that lived on the same coral never knew he was there.

Occhi had tried many times to change his colour.

Did you know that octopuses can do this *just by thinking?*

Occhi spent many days thinking.

His colours moved around when he thought: the pinky-grey bits changed into bluey-green bits and the greeny-blue bits changed into browny-mauve bits; but it didn't really make much difference to how he looked.

He waved with all his eight arms at the fishes and other creatures passing by ~ but no one ever saw him or came over to say, "What a beautiful home you have!" or even just to say, "Hello! Rather unsettled currents we're having today."

Occhi became more and more lonely, more and more sad, with no one to talk to and no one to play with.

Then, one day, a most strange thing happened.

High up above his home, above the salt seawater, above the waves, in a place that Occhi had only dreamed of, the sun was playing games with a shower of rain.

Together, the sun and the rain had decided to make a rainbow. Half of it swept up into the sky in an enormous arch shape. The other half of the rainbow delved deep down into the sea, right in front of Occhi's home. Occhi saw the bright strong bands of colour turn the water yellow, red, orange, blue, purple and green, with beautiful shades of colour in between.

"Oh! Oh! Oh! How wonderful! I want to be just like that!
There must be enough colours for each of my arms!"
(He was quite good at counting up to six).

It was very difficult for Occhi to change into these bright colours; he didn't know how to go about it.

He spent two weeks thinking orange ~ and nothing much happened.

He spent three weeks thinking purple ~ and nothing much happened.

He spent four weeks thinking blue ~ and nothing much happened.

Then he began to lose his patience and he became cross:

"It's not fair. I'm thinking and thinking so hard it's making my nine brains hurt and I'm still not changing colour."

He became angrier and angrier, just thinking how unfair it was ~ and angrier still, thinking how the whole wobbly world was unfair. As he got angrier, he noticed a very strong spot of red appearing near the end of arm number three. The spot seemed to be growing bigger and bigger and spreading outwards and upwards ~ a wonderful bright red ~ a red just like the one in the rainbow!

"Ooooooh!
So this is how you do it!"

So he thought "angry" some more and watched as the bright red crept up his arm, higher and higher.

Then he thought "angry" even more than before and soon arm number three was completely red ~ just as he had wanted. Then the red started to spread all over his wobbly body. Red tips were beginning to form at the ends of arms one, two, four, five, six, seven and eight ~ he would soon be completely red.

"No, no!
Too much!
Stop! Stop!!
I don't want to be a red-all-over octopus!"

Occhi made himself think a bit less "angry" and the redness started to fade.

Now he had the colour just where he wanted it and nowhere else; he had an attractive splash of red on his body and a red arm number three.

So what about the other colours?

Occhi started to experiment.

He tried thinking "gentleness and kindness". This was quite difficult, because he had to completely stop thinking "angry". He thought about lovely gentle things ~ the sea-horses with their tiny miniature foals and delicate sea-fronds dancing with the tides. Soon, a colour started to appear at the tip of arm number six. It was brilliant blue.

Then he tried thinking "happiness". This was easier for him, because he now felt so pleased with himself. A sunny egg-yolky yellow started creeping up arm number two.

Now he had the three most important colours.

Occhi spent the next six weeks experimenting with his new colours:

Lots of "feeling happy", with just a bit of "feeling angry",
gave him a delicious orange arm number one.

Large amounts of "feeling kind and gentle", with just a hint of
"isn't life unfair",
gave him a rich purple arm number five.

"Feeling pleased with himself" and "feeling gentle and kind"
gave him a gorgeous green arm number six

It was very complicated, having such a mixture of feelings all at the same time, even for an octopus with nine brains. Sometimes, the whole effect was ruined, because he had a bad day and became cross and frustrated. Quite suddenly, he would turn bright scarlet all over. But he learnt to calm himself down and think different thoughts. Deep breathing and yoga exercises helped to get rid of the red, so long as he didn't get his eight arms into a tangle.

~o~O~o~

Occhi and the Rainbow

Occhi grew older and older and spent day after day getting his body and arm colours just the way he wanted them.

Today, if you happen to swim past his home, you will see him waving to you with arms of every colour of the rainbow. He is the happiest, saddest, most gentle, most angry, thoughtful, melancholy, extrovert and carefree creature in the sea. He is never lonely, because ~ depending upon which arm he chooses to wave ~ he gets on with just about everyone!

Brief explanation:

In the course of my work as a theatre designer, I devised and led a practical workshop for primary school teachers, based around ideas for making fantastical sea creatures with household materials. One of our creations was a giant-sized octopus, made from a polystyrene bead-filled cushion with bubble-wrap tentacles. We also made puffer fish with tennis balls, sea anemones from mops and other strange animals and fish.

After this practical session with the teachers, I sat the octopus in an armchair and he seemed to take on a character of his own.

I developed this story following this experience. It is really intended to be performed by an adult ~ with the possibility of the children participating using other sea creatures that they have made, and for the giant "puppet" Occhi to be animated by the leader as he or she tells the story.

THE MAN IN THE GREY SUIT

Liz Haigh

Starting school wasn't too traumatic for me. I had an elder brother, Connor, who was two years older than me, so I already knew a lot about it, having been dragged along to take him and bring him home everyday for the last two years. The only slightly disconcerting part I remember is my first school assembly, with all 378 school children crammed in the school hall, the big ones at the back, the reception class at the front. We had strict instructions to stand still, always look to the front, no laughing or talking or we would have to stand outside. All the teachers were standing down the side of the hall. On the stage in front of us stood Mr Billings, our head teacher. Mr Wakefield, the deputy head, was to his right, and to his left stood an older man. It was some time before I found out this man's name, as he never spoke in assemblies. He just stood there looking at us all. I always remember that he wore a grey three-piece suit, with an old-fashioned watch and chain in his pocket.

It wasn't until nearly the end of the school year, when I went up to Mr Billings's office with some kids from my class to show him our art project, that I discovered the name of the Man in the Grey Suit who never spoke. There was a large black and white photograph of him above Mr Billings's desk. In the photograph, he looked very serious, almost unhappy, as if there was something he wanted to say. I must have been in an unusually bold mood that day, because I asked Mr Billings who the man was.

"That's Mr Sutton, the founding head teacher of this school. He was head teacher here for over thirty years," he replied.

"It's nice for him still to come to our assemblies," I said. I was rather confused when Mr Billings laughed and told me that Mr Sutton had been dead for over fifty years. I wanted to ask more questions, but was told to hurry back to class before the bell went.

I tried talking to Mum about it that night, while she was cooking tea. I was still too young to know that while she was getting tea ready was not the best time to ask difficult questions. Her reply was:

"What? Well, it must be someone who looks like him; a distant relative or something." Then she told me to wash my hands and set the table. She seemed happy with the explanation, so I was too.

So, for the next two years, I just did as I was told at school and never really bothered much about this Mr Sutton lookalike in assembly, who was always there, but never said anything. I never asked any of my friends about him or if they could see him. Maybe it would have been better if I had.

On the one hand, I would say that I will remember that winter assembly of my Year Three forever. On the other hand, the exact sequence of events will always be a little hazy. I remember clearly that I was standing towards the back of the hall, as I was getting to be one of the older boys now. My feet were wet through and cold, as I had been playing in the snow on my way to school. We had had the first heavy snowfall for several years and had all been throwing snowballs and generally messing around.

Mr Billings was, as usual, standing centre stage, with Mr Wakefield to his left and the ever silent Man in the Grey Suit to his right. Mr Billings was just telling us about how the Sponsored Spell had raised over £400 towards the school roof fund when something quite remarkable happened. The Man in the Grey Suit stepped forward and shouted in a loud, but calm and commanding, voice that we must all leave the hall at once: no rushing or pushing, youngest out first, the school roof is falling in. There was a lot of mumbling and noise, but everyone more or less did as they were told and filed out of the hall. For some reason, I was one of the last to leave, when the roof collapsed. The next thing I remember, I was in a hospital bed, with my parents, my brother Connor and Mr Billings all sitting by my bedside gaping at me.

What happened over the next few weeks is even more of a haze than the day of the accident itself. I tried explaining to my Mum that the Man in the Grey Suit had finally spoken and effectively evacuated the hall and saved everyone, but no one else seemed to have seen him. Eventually, I spoke to Connor about it, as he was there. He was in Year Six now and going to the Big School next year, so he was practically a grown-up. Surely he would have heard the Man in the Grey Suit evacuate the hall and get us all out before the roof fell in and killed us all. To my absolute astonishment, he said:

"No, it was you, Daniel, who ran on the stage and told us all to leave." He said it was me who saved everybody. This was all a bit too confusing. I still had a bump on my head, which hurt if I thought about things too much.

Eventually, my parents and I had a meeting with Mr Billings in his office. He seemed a little edgy. Apparently, the school governors needed a full explanation of the events of that winter assembly. Everyone was pleased that no one had been seriously hurt, but they were asking why an eight-year-old boy had been the one to take charge of the situation. Mr Billings was asking me about that morning, but then answering the questions for me before I could speak.

"You looked up at the ceiling before anyone else and saw it breaking up, didn't you, Daniel? Isn't that why you bravely acted as you did and got everyone out?"

The Man in the Grey Suit

I opened my mouth to say that it wasn't me, that it was the Man in the Grey Suit, but my head still hurt and I was tired, so I simply said, "Yes, Sir."

I was told that I was going to get my picture taken for the paper and given some sort of award, but was not much pleased by it. I felt like a fraud. It was only as we were getting up to leave that I finally looked at the large picture above Mr Billings's desk. It *was* the Man in the Grey Suit. It *was* Mr Sutton, but he was no longer looking so serious and grim. He was actually smiling and that made me smile.

School life from then on carried on pretty much as normal. In a few months, the new school hall roof was completed and school assemblies happily continued without any major incidents or event. I never again saw Mr Sutton in any of the school assemblies, but I didn't mind. I had the feeling the danger had passed. The school was safe and he had moved on. We could all move on.

LEATHERBACK

David Brazier

The turtle awoke.

What had disturbed her sleep she did not know; perhaps a quake on a distant seabed, or the throb of a ship's propellers, or some intuitive sense of the danger rising from below.

She dipped her head and peered into a plankton fog flickering with the light-pores of feeding lanternfish. Below the plankton bloom, a faint coloured glow was emanating from the depths, rapidly growing in radiance and intensity. The turtle raised her head to breathe, and the moonlit swell seemed to shatter into silver-green splinters as thousands of lanternfish erupted from the waves and rained back down.

The turtle dived, and barged through the dense confusion of fish until she broke into water sparkling with emerald diatoms[1] and the opalescent barrels of comb jellies.

Then salvoes of red and yellow rockets flared up from the depths as squid up to a metre long punched holes in the lanternfish shoal, clubbing and hooking, flailing and swatting, snaring and seizing, and then dropping away, their tentacles bucking with the ineffectual escape attempts of the prey wrapped within. Others hung vertically and dexterously filleted their food, discarding heads and guts, the water blood-clouded by their labours. The severed head of one large lanternfish dropped past the turtle's face,

---

[1] Microscopic organisms with a glass-like cell wall. They float in the levels of the sea that the sun reaches.

its luminous light pores still glowing, until it faded into black.

But the black wore ribbons of blue-green phosphorescence. As the turtle had found before, whenever squid massed in such numbers, the sharks would come.

The blue shark twitched. A shudder ran the length of his slender body and he surged upwards, tail sweeping hard and fast as he drove straight into the mass of squid and fish. Detonations of ink puffed all around the turtle as the squid took evasive actions - quicksilver fast, tight movements, swift changes of direction, sharp, sudden bursts of acceleration and abrupt stops.

Scores of sharks shot past the turtle and piled into the squid, slashing and snapping, popping some bodies and wolfing others whole. True gluttons of the sea, many gorged past their stomach's capacity, regurgitated what they had already taken and started feasting again.

The turtle banked hard and swam away, determined to put a safe distance between herself and the expanding frenzy. The blue sharks would not target her deliberately, but in their voracious haste they could snap at her flippers, or take a swipe at her head.

She stretched her flippers in preparation for a full power stroke, and froze. A tiger shark was stalking her, eyes glinting and glowing green outline tracing ever-tightening circles. The turtle fought the urge to bolt, knowing she could not outswim the shark and that any panic movements would entice and arouse him. The shark closed to within twelve metres of her and she could see the true size of the ocean prowler - at least four times her own length. The turtle held her nerve, carefully tilted both rear paddles, relaxed her fore flippers, and began to drop.

The tiger shark followed her, leisurely descending in a spiral of decreasing circles, seemingly content to wait and see what she would do before making his move.

At five hundred metres below sea level, the shark dropped beneath her – his favoured angle of attack. With her head drooped, the turtle watched the predator's approach, his sleek and powerful bulk sheathed in cold blue radiance and balanced waves of sinuous movement, culminating in precise sideways sweeps of his tail.

At six hundred metres, the shark moved in. His first exploratory pass was so close that the turtle felt the pressure change of his motion, and on the return pass she saw his gill slits flare, and felt the rasping kiss of a pectoral fin.

At seven hundred metres, the shark swept up and past once more, and tail-slapped the turtle's side, twirling her round, daring her to flee; but the turtle knew that any sudden movements would invite a ferocious and fatal attack, so she simply span and sank even faster.

At nine hundred metres, the shark headed directly for her and bumped her hard with his snout in the soft flesh of her throat pouch. She lurched backwards, then toppled over and dropped into darkness, her flippers bent upwards in the rapid momentum of her descent.

The turtle plunged through one thousand metres, the deepest she had ever been. The shark circled just above her and headed towards her again, but this time his approach was lazier and less determined, as if the darkness and the turtle's lack of response had dulled his interest.

At eleven hundred metres, the turtle tumbled through the midst of a black swarm, pulsing with bright blue and red spheres - the eyes and wing tips of a vast flock of vampire squid, flapping their spread cape fins, reluctantly breaking formation to allow her through. Her flipper tip poked a globular eyeball and the squid instantly ejected a brilliant blue mucus, filled with tiny glowing balls, a glitter storm which swirled all over her and quickly faded away.

At twelve hundred metres, the frigid water had a waxen opaqueness which confused the turtle's senses and frustrated her eyes. The few lights visible came from creatures which hunted and hid and bred and died here: flashes and bursts of red, blue and green, streaking and vanishing; bioluminescence[2] to identify and beckon, illuminate and threaten; puffs and clouds of precious light to communicate and challenge, deceive and escape.

At fifteen hundred metres, the coldest water the turtle had ever known burned her entire body. Her thick layer of insulating fat calloused and cracked, and fatigue-injecting cold gnawed through flesh and blood, chilling the new life developing in her reproductive tract. A vague spherical outline pulsed close by, eleven metres across - a deep crimson bell, rimmed in shocking pink and trailing twenty metre-long diaphanous[3] tentacles. The turtle dropped only inches away from it, her cold-slugged brain incapable of executing an evasive manoeuvre, unaware that the briefest touch of one shimmering venom sac would instantly fuse every nerve in her body.

At sixteen hundred metres, she briefly felt the sonar clicks of a sperm whale hunting below, their echoes sketching a sound map to guide him through abyssal canyons draped with the frozen flows of ancient lava.

At eighteen hundred metres, the crushing weight of water clamped the turtle's carapace tight against her plastron and her semi-rigid chest collapsed. Bitter cold stung and cramped her muscles, sucking the last trace of warmth from her blood, and she began to slide into unconsciousness.

---

[2] Light created by an organism.
[3] Translucent.

Word Weaving

At two kilometres below sea level, a mere one hundred metres above the sea floor, she sank towards a seabed carpeted with the summer's plankton bloom and grazed by herds of giant spider crabs. The sperm whale cruised by, his mouth held open as he tongue-squeezed squid between his teeth, aggravating his brilliant lure - a glowing cephalopod[4] paste which coated his teeth and glossed his lips, coaxing curious prey within range.

The turtle's flippers hung limp, unable to function on their meagre ration of cold blood and twitching uncontrollably as compressed nerves fired messages to redundant muscles. Her core body temperature was now so low that she was on the edge of toppling into a state of cold-stunning, and in a matter of moments she would be chill-crippled past the point of recovery. Another degree colder and her body would enter irreversible shutdown.

Suddenly, a loud clang vibrated through the water. Then another boom of sound, and another, closer still, shook her body. The sperm whale was nearing the end of his dive and hunting at maximum pace, casting his deepest tones to flick on lights in the bodies of unseen squid.

The next moment, the whale's cliff head filled the turtle's vision, his thick lips dribbling luminescence. Another concentrated burst of bass creaks sent needles of sound through her flesh and bone, penetrating her stupor, and in a sluggish, semi-conscious motion, she tilted and lurched upwards.

Twelve minutes later she burst through the surface, heave-breathing and gagging on partially digested jellyfish.

She fanned her flippers and paddled to stay afloat, shivering hard as warmth returned to her body. But with

---

[4] The scientific name for a family of sea creatures, which includes the squid and the octopus.

the return of feeling came overwhelming fatigue and a fierce, cold-induced hunger. But rest and nourishment would have to wait. First she had a beach to find, and a nest to dig, and eggs to lay.

She checked her bearings and then stretched and swept her front flippers, clumsily at first; but after a few strokes she settled into a fluid, consistent rhythm, an energy-efficient motion to carry her and her embryos westward across a thousand kilometres of ocean and beyond - to the Gulf of Oman and the beach of her birth.

THE WORM, THE TELLY AND THE NIGHTINGALE

Nick Buchanan

Stanley was up in his room playing with his toys when suddenly there was a bright flash and he was turned into a worm. How it happened he didn't know. He slithered downstairs to tell his dad.

"Dad, it's me. I've been turned into a worm," he said.

His dad looked at him from around the side of his newspaper. "We don't have worms in our house," he said. Then he picked the worm up and took it to the back garden.

"But Dad, it's me. Stanley." He tried to point to himself as he said it, but he didn't have any arms.

"You don't fool me," said his dad. "You may be a clever worm, but you're not allowed on our carpets!" Mr Barker threw the worm on to some soil. Then he returned to his newspaper. After a short while, he called to his wife in the kitchen.

"Daphne!"

"Yes, dear?"

"Where's Stanley? Shouldn't he be home by now?"

"He is. He's up in his room."

"Oh. Right."

Just then Mr Barker heard an item on the 'News' that made him put his paper down and listen: "... *and in the North West, particularly the Wirral region, some things may change into other things. Scientists are not yet sure of the reason for this, but they are working on it. We'll let you know more as news comes in.*" Hmmm, thought Mr Barker. "*Some things may change into other things.*" Now what do they mean by that?

He called to his wife again. "Daphne!"

The Worm, the Telly and the Nightingale

Daphne hurried in from the kitchen, wiping her hands on her apron. "Yes, dear, what is it?"

"On the 'News', they said that *some things may change into other things*". Now what do you make of that?"

"Well, it does sound a little odd, dear. Turn the channel over and see if there's anything about it on the other side."

He picked up the remote control and pressed a button. The television immediately turned into a dog. A real dog, that was sitting, looking back at them.

"Ouh , it's never done that before," Daphne said. "Shall I get the repair man?"

"No. It won't need repairing. It's ….It's a dog now; but it *will* need feeding. Don't you see? It's what they said on the 'News': *'Some things may change into other things.'*"

"All right, dear," said Mrs Barker, putting on her scarf and coat. "You stay here and I'll go out and get some dog food for the telly."

Mr Barker tried to settle down once more to read his paper, but the new dog started scratching at the back door and whining. "All right! All right! Honestly! We never had to let you out when you were a telly!" He opened the back door and the dog ran playfully into the back garden. Mr Barker returned to his chair and his newspaper.

Outside, the dog was sniffing around when he came upon the loose soil where Mr Barker had thrown the worm. He started digging, but then he saw Stanley.

"Stop!" shouted the worm. "I may look like a worm, but I'm really a boy called Stanley."

"Don't worry," said the dog. "I may look like a dog, but I'm really a telly: the one from your living room."

"Wow!" said Stanley. "How did that happen?"

"I'm not sure," said the dog. "But when I was a telly, there was a 'News' item that said, *'Some things might change into other things.'*"

71

"I suppose we've become two of those 'other things,'" said Stanley.

"Yep!" said the dog.

Just then, Daphne came out into the back garden with some dog food in a bowl. "Here you are," she said. She set it down, then went back inside.

"Would you excuse me a minute?" the dog said to the worm. "I may really be a telly, but I'm feeling very hungry, and that dog food looks delicious."

"Go ahead," said the worm. "I need some time to think anyway".

Inside the house, Daphne came rushing downstairs. "Where's Stanley?" she said.

"I don't know," said Mr Barker.

"Do you think it's got anything to do with things becoming other things - like our telly becoming a dog?"

And then Mr Barker remembered the worm earlier. "Oh, dear! Oh, no! I should have .... "

"What is it, dear?" said Daphne.

"I think our Stanley's a worm now."

"A worm?"

"Yes. And he's only about that long." He held his finger and thumb apart. "I put him in the back garden."

"With the dog? He could be eaten!" They both rushed out into the back garden, where they found the dog with the worm on the end of his nose.

"Put him down! Don't eat him! He may look like a worm to you, but he's my son!" screamed Mr Barker.

"He wants to ride on my nose," said the dog.

"I didn't know he could talk," said Daphne. "Mind you, he must have picked up a lot of words when he was a telly!"

"Who cares!" said Mr Barker sharply. "Right now, all I want to do is help get our son back to normal." Then he bent down and looked closely at the worm on the dog's nose.

"Listen, Dad," said the worm. "He let me get up on his nose to keep me from getting trodden on. We'll find a way out of this, if we just calm down and think it through. You mustn't be unkind to the dog. Remember all the happy hours you spent sitting in front of him when he was a telly."

"I'll make a cup of tea," said Daphne. "It'll settle us all and we'll be able to think better." She went indoors.

Mr Barker sat at the garden table, folded his arms, and looked defeated. "I just don't know what we're going to do."

The dog came up and put his nose on Mr Barker's knee and was given a stroke behind the ears. The worm on the dog's nose looked up. "Dad, I want you to think back to the moment when our telly turned into this dog."

"Okay," said Mr Barker, closing his eyes. "Let me see. I remember now. I was sitting in my favourite telly chair, ..."

"Yes?" said the worm. "And did you do anything that made the telly change, or did it just change by itself?"

"Well, I just pressed the remote control and, ... "

"That's it! Go and get the remote!" said the worm, bobbing up and down on the dog's nose. Mr Barker ran in to get it.

Daphne came out with the mugs of tea on a tray. She barely had time to set them down when Mr Barker came rushing out again, waving the remote in his hand. "Here we are!"

"Okay," said the worm. "Point it at the dog, and press the same button that you pressed when it changed into a dog."

Mr Barker held the remote out at arms length and pressed the button marked '1'. There was no puff of smoke or flash or anything like you see in magic shows, but suddenly there was no dog; just a TV set with a worm on top.

Mrs Barker clapped her hands with joy. "We've got our telly back. Just think how much we'll save on dog food now!"

"And we can sit and watch it now. It's no good watching a dog!" said Mr Barker. Then he looked at the worm. "Now, if only I knew a way to get our Stanley back."

"Try button '2,'" suggested Daphne.

"How do you mean?" said Mr Barker.

"Well, button '1' got us our telly back. Button '2' might get us our Stanley back."

"I suppose it's worth a try." Mr Barker pointed the remote at the worm and pressed button '2'. Suddenly Stanley was there, sitting on top of their telly, his face dirty with soil.

"Stanley!" Daphne ran forward and gave him a big hug.

"I love you, Mum," said Stanley.

"And we love you too," said Daphne.

Mr Barker wiped some dog food pieces off the top of the telly. "And I can't wait to get this plugged in again," he said.

Daphne elbowed him sharply and nodded towards Stanley. "Oh, of course!" he said. "Yes, it's good to have you back, too. We *do* love you, son."

Stanley, his mum and his dad all hugged together. They didn't notice that their nosy neighbour, Mrs Burridge, was looking over the fence; until she spoke, of course.

"It's not love he needs," she said. "It's a good, hard smack. Dragging your telly outside and sitting on it. Look at that soil on his face. He's a filthy boy. A cheeky, dirty animal, if you ask me. And what does he think he's doing, bringing your TV outdoors, anyway? It might have been raining. He could've electrocuted us all, he could, with no thought, ..."

"Actually, it wasn't like that," said Mr Barker.

He was going to say more, but Mrs Burridge started off again. " ... and I mean, it's not as if he doesn't know right from wrong. He just chooses to be bad every time!"

"He hasn't done anything wro ...." Daphne didn't get a chance to finish.

"Next thing," Mrs Burridge went on, "it'll be *my* telly in the garden and *my* family all electrocuted, and then, before you know it, the whole street will ...." Mrs Burridge droned on and on and sounded as if she'd never stop.

But she did stop. She stopped immediately, because Mr Barker pointed the remote control at her and pressed button '3'.

Hurriedly, Stanley and his mum and dad went indoors, carrying the telly. When they switched it on, it worked fine. The first thing they saw was a newsreader saying, *"And we now hear that things are no longer changing into other things. From now on everything will stay just as it is."*

That was a relief to all of them. And it was good news for Mrs Burridge, because she sounds much nicer now than she ever did when she was person. It would be a shame now if she ever changed back.

Stanley puts seeds out for her in winter and he makes sure she's got a drink. But he never feeds her worms, even though she likes them. Mr Burridge found out, of course, but he says he prefers her this way.

Now that she's a nightingale.

JABULANI AND THE MEANING OF LIFE

Merle Colborne

When Jabulani was little and wore nothing but a cotton vest to cover his small round belly, he would sit on the old man's lap and gaze into the kindly face, scribbled with the joy and pain of many years, listening to the legends and stories of his people. Though he did not understand all the words, he loved the sound of them and the way the sentences rose and fell with Tatamkhulu's breath as he spoke.

And, from the time Jabulani started school in the long short pants he so proudly put on, until he finished in the short long pants he so shamefully wore, he would stop and talk to the old man and would feel the contentment that seemed to drape about him like the mists on the morning hills.

It was only natural then that, when the letter came, Jabulani should run and show the old man.

"Look, Tatamkhulu! I have completed my education," he said, and great was the excitement in his voice.

The old man's smile was slow.

"See, Tata!" Jabulani showed him the thick sheet of paper with the gold printing and his name written in black ink.

"It is a fine thing, this paper," said the old man. "It means that you know some things from some books that some people think you should know. But," he added, tapping both his head and his heart, "it doesn't mean that you are finished with learning."

"What do you mean, Tata?" asked Jabulani, his voice heavy with disappointment.

Jabulani and the Meaning of Life

"Can you tell me the Meaning of Life?" asked the old man.

Jabulani thought for a while. If I say one thing, the old man will say another. And if I say another thing, the old man will come up with a third.

"No," he said finally.

"That is a wise answer," said the old man "Knowing that you don't know is the beginning of wisdom."

"So what is the Meaning of Life?" asked Jabulani, well pleased with himself.

"That you will have to find out!" said Tatamkhulu.

"But how, Tata?" asked the boy.

"You must go on a journey and the people you meet and the things you see, the creatures in the bush and the birds in the sky, the women by the river and the river too - they will tell you. And when you know the answer, you must come back and tell me."

So the boy went home and told his mother what the old man had said.

"The Meaning of Life?" his mother laughed. "The Meaning of Life is to get a job!"

But, because she loved him and knew the old man was wise, she gave him her blessing, and the money she had saved over many months for a suit with trousers neither too long nor too short for his first day of work.

And so Jabulani set off.

He asked the mountains: "What is the Meaning of Life?" and the mountains replied majestically "Life - Life - Life," which might have been an echo or might have been an answer.

He asked a man sitting crossed legged on the slope "Aummmmmmm," said the man.

He asked the stream, but the stream, running to join the river, just babbled.

He asked the river, all in a rush, which gushed, "Life is flow. Or flux." - which is what an old Greek man said two and a half thousand years before.

The river bank, hearing the question, slipped in an answer: "Life is having things pass you by."

"Nonsense!" said an old woman weaving a basket from the reeds growing by the river. "Life is what you make it."

So he asked the young woman walking along a rocky path with a bucket on her head. "Life!" she laughed, as the water sloshed and slapped the metal sides. "Life is a container. What you put in is what you get out."- which is what the Duke of Edinburgh, who lives in Buckingham Palace with his wife the Queen, once said. "But there are times," laughed the woman as she stumbled, "that Life is a waste."

Sometimes, as he travelled these paths, Jabulani carried a sadness in his heart for his mother and for his brothers and sisters, and for the father he had hardly known."

But the sky consoled him with a sunny smile, saying: "It is only when you know what it is to be blue that you can really know what happiness is."

"Yes," said the beggar, who had the answer in the palm of his hand. "Life is a coin with two faces."

"But it's what's in the middle that really counts," proffered the sandwich seller.

"Life is humbug!" said an old professor and gave him a sweet.

"No, it's a mess!" said an officer tucking into a meal.

"And a muddle!" said the woman sorting out the washing.

Jabulani had been travelling many days and many miles, but felt no closer to answering the old man's question.

So he put it to the lake and the lake calmly replied: "The Meaning of Life is to live to the full." But the stone

Jabulani flung into the water warned, "Life is the ripples that spread from all our actions!" and disappeared.

"Life is a breeze," said a small wind in the trees.

"Nonsense," said the rock. "Life is hard."

Then he came to a cave and asked his question again, but the cave just yawned and said, "I'm in the dark."

But the artist working at the rock face said, "Life is something you draw from inside you."

"No," said the dung beetle on a roll. "Life is just the same old thing day after day after day after day."

Jabulani asked a crow, who said he would show him directly and flew off in a straight line.

So he asked the owl. "To woo," said the owl, hooting as he set off on his date.

"Life is adapting to change," said the chameleon, turning scarlet.

Sometimes, as he looked at the horizon, Jabulani wondered whether the Meaning of Life was something always out of reach.

Then, one day, in the rondavel[1] of a Xhosa[2] man, he heard a high-pitched whistling from the mud walls. He had heard that sound before.

And the Xhosa man said, "That is the sound of the Nomatotlo, the small spirits that go all over the world to gather knowledge and bring it to you."

Then Jabulani remembered: he had heard that sound in the room where the school computer was kept. "But you have to know how to get them to give you that knowledge," the old man continued.

"Just like the Internet," said the boy, very excited, but the Xhosa man did not hear him.

---

[1] A round hut with a thatched roof.

[2] The African people who come from the Eastern Cape. Nelson Mandela is Xhosa.

So Jabulani went to a cyber café and the Internet said, "Search me!"

And Jabulani began to wonder if indeed that was what he should do, but then he thought about Tatamkhulu. If the answer could be found in one place, then why did the old man send him on a journey?

And then one evening, as he walked side by side with a Khoi Khoi man in the long leaning of the light, the man stopped and told the boy to take several paces forward. "Then you will be free. No man should walk in the shadow of another. Like all things that are born and all things that die, like all things that blossom and all things that fade, you have a right to be on this earth and to be who you are, which is unlike anyone else." And he bade him goodbye and a safe journey home.

Jabulani's mother was overjoyed to see the son so dear to her heart and began preparing a welcome feast. But first Jabulani had to go and see Tatamkhulu.

With the passing of the days, the old man's hair had turned the colour of the thorns that adorned the mimosa trees in the summer heat, and with the passing of the nights, the old man's eyes had turned the colour of the moon when it hung in the winter air.

And the old man took Jabulani's hand.

"I have been expecting you, my son." he said. "Now, tell me. What is the Meaning of Life?"

And Jabulani waited a moment and then he took a deep breath and began. "I saw many things, Tata, and met the creatures of the earth and the birds of the sky, the women who worked in the country and the men who lived in the cities, but each one had a different answer." And he told him all that he had experienced.

And when he had finished, the old man asked, "And all this time when you were asking your question, what were you doing?"

"Nothing, Baba. Just living."

"Aha!" said the old man. "So you do know the answer."

And he gave a deep contented sigh, for his days left on this earth were not many.

THE CORKSCREW

Maggie Spooner

These are the seabirds that Man killed.

This is the coast so empty and wild
That sheltered the birds that Man killed.

This is the tide of surge and slack
That lapped the coast
That sheltered the birds that Man killed.

This is the oil so stinking and black
That fouled the tide of surge and slack
That lapped the coast so empty and wild
That sheltered the birds as they dabbled and dived,
The beautiful birds that Man killed.

This is the ship, a rusty tub,
That leaked the oil so stinking and black
That fouled the tide of surge and slack
That lapped the coast so empty and wild
That sheltered the birds as they dabbled and dived,
The beautiful birds that Man killed.

This is the rock that lay offshore
 (By a hidden reef on the ocean floor)
That holed the ship
That leaked the oil so smelly and black
That fouled the tide of surge and slack
That lapped the coast so empty and wild
That sheltered the birds as they dabbled and dived,
The beautiful birds that Man killed.

The Corkscrew

This is the fog that descended at dawn
That hid the reef on the ocean floor
That holed the tanker and broke its back
And spilled the oil so stinking and black
That came with the tide of surge and slack
That lapped the coast so empty and wild
And poisoned the birds who couldn't survive,
The beautiful birds that Man killed.

This is the Captain all draggled and drawn
Who cursed the fog that descended at dawn
That hid the rock
That holed the ship
That spilled the oil
That came with the tide
That lapped the coast so empty and wild
And poisoned the birds who couldn't survive,
All the beautiful birds that Man killed.

These are the bottles of cheap Bordeaux
That fuddled the captain and made him slow
As he cursed the fog
That hid the rock
That holed the ship and broke its back
And leaked the oil so evil and black
That came on the tide of surge and slack
And lapped the shore so empty and wide
And coated the birds who couldn't survive,
All the beautiful birds that Man killed.

This is the corkscrew of cunning design
That opened the bottles of cheap red wine
That fuddled the Captain and got him pissed
As he cursed the blanket of blinding mist

Word Weaving

That hid the rock that lay offshore,
That treacherous reef on the ocean floor,
That holed the tanker and broke its back
And leaked the oil so evil and black
That came on the tide of surge and slack
That lapped the coast so empty and wild
And poisoned the birds in its waters wide,
The innocent birds who struggled and died,
The beautiful birds that Man killed.

And just before they abandoned ship
A steward came through and noticed it
And he went to the rail and stood and threw it
- And Davy Jones is welcome to it.

CHARLIE'S MOUSE

Sheila M. Blackburn

Charlie crouched behind the bins.

He folded himself up where the greyness smelled of old wee and his anger heaved out in great, hurting gasps. His face was sweating dirty-hot-red and his little fists thumped and bruised on the tarmac.

Out there, where the sun pressed down burning hard, the big kids still played in the dust on the gum-pocked pavements. But they didn't want Charlie.

"Gerroff our pirate ship!" they snarled. And Charlie stood on the grey-black grid and looked for a boat with white sails and tall masts.

"There's no ship here." He shrugged at the simple truth of it. For there *was* only the grey-black grid, with its shiny-dark bumps and the letters that he couldn't read.

Jake-From-Over-the-Street snarled and waved a homemade cutlass.

"Walk the plank!"

They grabbed him then and pulled him by the arms, and their sweat-angry shouts were right in his face.

"But there isn't a plank!" his small voice protested.

He didn't get their game and they didn't get what he was up to. As if he was calling them liars. A bigger boy would have been more fun. But Charlie was skinny-small and didn't know how to argue.

"You're rubbish," they said. "Just rubbish! Get lost!"

So Charlie took himself to the rubbish place – the big skips behind the shops. Only, *he* called them bins. Skips were jumpy-hoppy things you did with your feet. These were bins - where the rubbish went. And Charlie was rubbish. The big kids had said so.

Charlie sighed. It was a deep sigh that wobbled somewhere in his throat. He lifted a fist to his mouth and licked at the blood-crazed skin of his knuckles.

It was hard. Everything was *so* hard. He tried to be a good boy. He tried to understand, but sometimes it was just too hard.

Well, most of the time, actually.

Like in the mornings, when Mum said, "Come *on*, Charlie. Get a move on."

He wanted to be a good boy. He wanted to do it. But she hadn't told him what "a move" was – she hadn't shown him one – so how could he get one and put it on?

Sometimes he stood and stared, frozen in his own mind, wanting to know so much, but not having the words. And she'd rush around and say things like, "Pull yourself together, Charlie," and it made no sense at all.

As far as he could see, he *was* together, all in one piece. He didn't need pulling together, and she knew he didn't like being pulled or touched at all. She knew it, but not in the mornings, when she was all hairspray and rush-smeared lipstick.

"Don't just stand there, Charlie – *do* something!"

So he'd get out his best toy car, the one with the flashing headlights that went "on/off", "on/off", "on/off", "on/off", or smash at his Sugar Puffs with a spoon until the milk and sticky bits flew around - and then the shouting would start.

Charlie didn't like shouting, so he'd put his hands over his ears and hum a silly tune, until his ears buzzed and his heart boomed. Much better, he'd hide somewhere dark and secret, like he was hiding now.

Hiding was best. Being small and secret was safest and best.

"Hi, Charlie!"

Charlie squinted into the shadows.

"Hello?"

"Here. I'll climb up so you can see me." There was a small scuffling. A little brown mouse clambered on to Charlie's trainer. It waved at him and grinned.

"Oh – hello," Charlie said again. He was not surprised to find a mouse here in his new secret place – or a mouse talking, for that matter. Plenty of mice could talk. He'd seen them on TV.

"Glad you could make it."

"I didn't make anything," Charlie said, thinking Lego would have been better than the not-pirate-ship.

The mouse tried again. "Right. I mean - glad you dropped in."

"No - I squashed behind the bins; there's a dippy-down bit. I didn't drop."

The mouse had begun cleaning his rather fine, long whiskers. "That's OK, Charlie," he said easily. "That's cool. Nice to see you."

"Thank you," Charlie said, remembering his manners. "Do you live here, Miss Mouse?"

"It's Mr," corrected the mouse with a little cough. "And, yes, I do live here - for a bit."

"A bit of what?"

The mouse pulled at his whiskers, thoughtfully. "I'll be here for a few days," he said carefully, "until things get sorted."

"I can do sorting," Charlie told him.

"Good - welcome on board."

"Not the not-pirate-ship again!" Charlie groaned.

"Charlie – I mean, it's good to have your help."

Charlie wrinkled his nose. "I do wish people would say what they mean," he grumbled. "I get so mixed up."

"That's *people* for you, Charlie - I think you'll find mice are different!"

Charlie laughed.

87

"*Can* I help you?" he asked. "I like helping. Mum says I'm good at helping."

"Hmmmm," said the mouse and drummed his little claws on Charlie's trainer. "It's *your Mum* who needs sorting."

He watched Charlie carefully.

After a thinking time, Charlie said, "I don't sort mums. I sort blocks and plastic Teds – and money."

"Understood, Charlie. But this time you can sort things out for your Mum – and *my* Mum too!"

"Wow!"   Charlie jiggled and the mouse nearly tipped off his trainer-perch. "How?"

The mouse smiled. He had some explaining to do – carefully.

"Well," he began,

"Yes, thank you," said Charlie."

The mouse stared at Charlie with kindly eyes. "You just listen, Charlie. I'll tell you when you should speak again. OK?"

Charlie nodded.

The mouse took a deep breath. His mother would have scoffed at *this* helper. "That boy," she'd have sniffed, "he's a right Charlie!" But there was no time to be picky.

"Charlie – you know your Mum's got a problem – and I don't mean you. I mean, she thinks there are mice in your house - and she wants to get rid of them?"

Charlie's eyes grew wide and he nodded.

"She's right – there *are* mice in her house – some of my family, in fact. We were just, er, passing through, when Mother got trapped - not in a mouse trap, thank goodness - in some sort of red-hidden-away-box - goodness knows what it was - but we couldn't nibble our way in and Mother couldn't nibble her way out. So you see, Charlie, your Mum wants us to get out - and we want to get out - and that's where you come in."

88

Charlie pulled a face.

"You can speak now," the mouse told him.

"My Mum was mad with me," Charlie said. Lots of things were fitting into place in his head.

"She said I was being bad - and she had a lot of work to do - and mice in the house. And she had to ring the mouse-man - and I thought she meant a man that looks like a mouse - and that was scary - and she said I could go and play with the big kids - and I did."

"And then you came here."

Charlie nodded and kept right on nodding while he did some big thinking.

The mouse waited.

"That's pretty big thinking, Charlie," he said at last.

"It's big, but not very pretty," Charlie whispered.

"And?"

"And I don't know about how to sort the mums - which colours and sorting trays do I get?"

The mouse closed his eyes.

"Not a problem," he explained gently. "Do you think you know this red-hidden-away-box, Charlie?"

"Yep - it's under my bed. A Lego box with a long pipe - and I put in a trapdoor." he added proudly.

"Smart," said the mouse with a shudder.

"It will be if I get some stickers to put on it."

"The thing is," interrupted the mouse, "can you get it - secretly - and bring it here - and rel.... er, let Mother go?"

"Secretly?" Charlie whispered.

"Very," nodded the mouse.

"And that's sorting mums, is it?"

"It most certainly is," said the mouse.

"I'll do it!" Charlie said and scrambled to his knees, so that the mouse went skittering away under a bin. "Sorry - you wait here - I'll be back."

Charlie did get back -- but not until the burning-hard sun had set and the evening shadows had spread long fingers along the street and under the bins.

Charlie sat behind the bins and listened to the voices – Mum and all the big kids and lots of others that he knew.

He sat behind the bins and saw the torch beams dancing and stretching into the coming night.

He sat behind the bins and hugged the red Lego box with the pipe and the trapdoor - and Mother Mouse twitching and scrabbling and sliding inside.

It had been his own adventure – miles better than the not-pirate-ship. A secret and safe and hidden away adventure in all his own special hiding places.

That's how Charlie had sorted the mums, without anyone seeing him.

Until…

"He's here - we can see him."

And, just as the big kids pulled at the bins - Charlie tugged the lid off the Lego box.

"Oh, Charlie!"

He turned his face to the torch-eyes looking down at him.

"I'm rubbish," Charlie said, happily. "I got lost - and I got sorted - and I'm good at helping and - I'm a good boy."

"Good boy," said a soft voice in the shadows. "Thank you."

ROMANY

Libby Harris

Lindsey stopped. The others walked on, giggling, poking, generally messing about. The tiers of their gypsy skirts flounced provocatively towards the group of lads they had spotted lounging against a banged-up old car to one side of the field. Gemma heaved with laughter, and bent her chest forward very deliberately in a convulsion of self-congratulation at finding the lads.

"C'mon, Linz." She flicked her eyes, expectantly, back at Lindsey, left standing beside a fairground tent.

Lindsey did not move, but something moved inside the tent. A minute ago they had all been game to have their fortunes told, but the boys had caught their eyes. Lindsey's eyes were transfixed on the shabby tarpaulin of the tent. Its panels were stitched together with hemp. It smelt of old oil, like a lock-up she had been in once. The tent was out of place; even here, at the Horse Fair, tents had been transplanted by trailers, or tarted up with red-striped plastic awnings.

"Lin-z-ee." Gemma's voice drawled in a lazy, American blockbuster accent. She had taken a cigarette from her cute little beaded handbag, raised it to her lips, ready to pout and pose for the boys. She was baffled by Lindsey's disinclination to move back into the sunlight, away from the scabby old tent. Gemma could easily bring Lindsey to heel; she had a dozen mean, taut little voices in her head to choose from – her mother's, her teachers', her older sister's - but the boys would hear her lose her cool and then they'd lose interest. Instead she asked Lindsey for a light.

91

But Lindsey could not move, would not move. Her heels dug into the beaten earth. She forced her face back towards the tent, where in the dark – snorting, like an animal - something shifted its position. Something beckoned.

It was hot; unusually so for Appleby. Stagnant. Nothing happened here when you were young, not even summer. Tourists came, but they looked through locals with ice-cream eyes. Lindsey wanted something to happen – something of her own making. She should go to the boys, be what they wanted her to be. There was a thrill to be had there. The words fell hollow in her head. This was a big lie. The boys were stupid, so you had to pretend to be even more stupid, or they wouldn't fancy you. The deep, dark chasm of the tent beckoned.

The field sloped down to a shallow boundary hedge. It was a good spot for dumping a wrecked car. You could give it a push from the dirt track at the top and watch it plough into the bank at the bottom. The lads had spotted the girls. They left off lounging and were ripping saplings from the hedge, beating them hard against the chassis of the old car, until bits of rust flaked into the air. They looked shorter than Lindsey knew they were; they looked like little boys, aimless; "gormless," her Gran would say. She pushed inside the tent in disgust.

"Ten pound." The voice was as dark as the tent was gloomy.

"That's all I've got." Lindsey heard her own voice in reply, but it sounded too thin, too plaintive.

"'know that already. Well, want your fortune, or what?"

After the bright sunlight, it took a time for Lindsey's eyes to adjust, and her senses were too busy with the smells inside the tent to make a good job of restoring her eyesight. It was not a repulsive smell exactly - but strong -

strong like peppermint - and the Vic Inhaler that her dad used - but rougher. Her eyes smarted, but she could breathe better. She felt suddenly awake, awake in the presence of something very strong and very old.

A person was turning playing cards on to a small table. Lindsey had never seen anyone so old; even sheep farmers looked young compared to *that*. The downturned face was so creased, the mouth so puckered, Lindsey nearly laughed; it was like looking at a cartoon of an old person, a shrivelled gumboot, an old rock cake with the currants sunk too far into the dough. Hadn't *it* ever heard of moisturiser? Of Factor 45? How much botox would it take to put *that* right? Kate Moss couldn't look like that if she lived to be a thousand.

The ancient thing lifted its head, but continued to work its hands in dealing the cards. The eyes were staring, cruelly. Lindsey raised herself to leave.

"Haven't got ten pounds."

"Right pocket of your jeans. Not got one of them pretty skirts, then?"

"You're freaky." Lindsey lifted the tenner from her jeans pocket.

"'m not one of your gypsies off the telly - all posh hair and blue eyeshadow, you know. I'm a true Romany. One of the blessed people, blessed with knowledge of what has been and what is to come. Ten pound - a' don't take less. 'm worth ten times your measly tenner. Pure Romany. No mixed blood in me ...."

The reply struck Lindsey as curious, more so than the old girl knowing where she kept her money. What did she mean about mixed blood? What did that have to do with anything? Was she racist or what? There were Asian girls at school, and Monica - her parents were Afro-Caribbean. Romany's skin was as dark as theirs, almost. Of course she was Black, or she'd done a lot of sunbathing. But the old girl was more exotic than that; she was the colour of earth.

Romany cackled. She had no teeth, just a gaping black hole.

"Ever seen a coloured with eyes like these?" She knew what Lindsey had been thinking. She turned the full beam of her eyes on Lindsey. Striking blue, green, grey; they defied description. Colour was not what these eyes were for. They were shards of piercing light that searched your soul, not seeing baubles to frame with mascara and pretty-up your face.

Lindsey pushed the money across the table. Romany raised it to the weak Cumbrian sun, which crept through the crack in the tarpaulin door, checking the detail of the Queen's picture.

"My name is Pearl. *You* can call me that." The ten pounds had softened the old girl; her voice flowed like thick cream and the words were uttered in such a way that Lindsey felt privileged - like the cat that got the cream. Her shoulders relaxed.

"And you are Lindsey." You could have got that from Gemma, screaming my name up the field, thought Lindsey. She watched the tenner slip down off the table into Pearl's lap.

"Lindsey Carpenter. You're a girl what wants to be a woman." Pearl raised her eyes once more from the cards as she spoke.

Lindsey's throat tightened again. This was not comfortable. She wondered how far the others had gone by now. Had they reached the boys? Had they left the Horse Fair altogether?

"Tell me what you see – quickly. I've got to catch up with my friends." Lindsey tried to sound cool, though she could never be as cool as this old crone.

94

"*Friends*, are they?" Pearl looked down at the cards then.

"Death." she said, simply, firmly.

"What?"

"Death. I see death. You wanted it quick. I see death."

Lindsey protested, the panic rising now in direct proportion to the old woman's matter-of-fact calm: "**Stop it. STOP** saying that. You're not supposed to say things like that - not to children anyway."

"Why? 'Swat I see. Wan' me to tell you, 'He's tall, dark and handsome,' is it? 'Snot there."

Lindsey didn't understand the reference. Her Gran might have. She guessed it meant "fit" - that she was going to meet a fit boy. Best way to do that was to leave this smelly hole of a tent now. The boys were outside by the car. Mucking about. Having a laugh. Not sitting here having some mad old bat tell them they were going to die.

"Romanies don't lie, little girl. I see **death**," she insisted sharply, and there was the end of a shriek lingering in her old throat. She pushed the ten pound note back at Lindsey. "If you don't want to hear, then take your filthy money. It's stolen anyhow. *I* don't touch dirty money." She turned her eyes to the table and continued to deal cards.

Lindsey was shaking, shivering. The old woman didn't lie. She didn't have to. She knew everything. She could read everything that was in Lindsey's head. Lindsey's voice came out very quietly.

"My Mother owed it me. I took it, but she would have given it to me if I'd asked."

Pearl lifted her head and halted her dealing: "That's better. You're listening now. What I see is what I see. Doesn't mean it's got to happen. Otherwise, what'd be the point in Him giving me the Gift? You were meant to come to my tent today, not go off with your friends. I was meant to help - that's all it means. You can have the tenner back.

If we meet again, it'll be you helping me - with those hands."

She stared across with the seeing eyes at the cool white hands in Lindsey's lap. "You've got healin' hands - a doctor's hand - a surgeon's hands."

"Me? A doctor?"

Pearl raised an eyebrow and grinned: "But it won't be no *plastic* surgery I'll be after."

Pearl cackled, and Lindsey laughed with her, a mad laugh, and she didn't know why. She felt very old and very tired, like Pearl must be feeling in the cramped dark tent, with its cold, grass carpet.

"You're beautiful," she said, and meant it.

"'Course I am," ricocheted the reply, and they laughed aloud again, not giving a damn for anyone.

There was an explosion. It was sudden. It was cold. The sides of the tent blew against the girl. She was out of her seat in a flash. People ran down the field. Men were shouting; harsh cries rent the summer air. Pearl stood alongside, her arm around Lindsey's waist; she was only half Lindsey's height, but solid as a rock.

The old car was ablaze; the petrol tank had been set on fire and belched black smoke upwind. People were hurt. Lindsey would have been hurt. In time, a fire engine would arrive, police, an ambulance.

Lindsey leant against Pearl and breathed camphor, cinnamon, juniper, wintergreen. She understood now the draw of the tent and why mucking about around that old car was the last place to be if you wanted a future. She had, at last, the sight.

THE GREEN MAN

Eleanor Pownall

Geraint runs. He runs so hard that it feels as if his chest is bursting, his organs pulsing and struggling to punch their way out. He runs uphill, feeling the veins in his neck throbbing and his breath coming in short, shallow rasps. With every heartbeat a scene flashes behind his eyelids, a sudden blood-washed snapshot of the past. He runs from the gates of the schoolyard, trainers thumping on the pavement and then skids round a wooden footpath sign on to the dusty track to the hill above the town. He can feel them behind him.

"To me! This way, you idiot!" Geraint stood panting in the middle of the Sports Hall, with the basketball clutched to his chest.

"Geraint, you prat, here!" spat James, his face in a fury. A dozen faces swam before Geraint's eyes and their voices merged into a slow muffled roar. He was sinking underwater, sinking lower and lower until there was nothing but the rushing in his ears.

"Geraint? Geraint?" Mr Adams's voice dragged him back. "Do you need your inhaler? Do you want to sit this one out?"

Geraint shook his head, turned away and threw up all over the floor.

He feels every thud pound through the soles of his feet, shoot up his legs, to his hips and reverberate in the hollows of his bones. The steps echo back down into the sandy ground beneath him, behind him, letting them feel how close he is. He runs up the sandy path, along the edge of the hills deeper into the woodland and up, always further up, straining with every step as they holler behind him.

He is dizzy with sickness, faint with the dull throb in his temples.

Last period in English class. He was sitting halfway back, near the window on the right, looking out over the chimneys of the power plant where his father had worked. The works was stranded, marooned by the grey ribbons of the estuary. It was already getting dark. To his left, hidden by the classroom wall, Helsby Hill jutted upwards from the high street.

"Le Morte d'Arthur," read out Miss Deed, as she copied the words on to the whiteboard and then turned to the class. "Now who can tell me anything about the legends of Arthur?" She was met with bored silence. James drummed his fingers on the table loudly and leant his chair right back, so it touched Geraint's desk.

"Now who knows the Knights of the Round Table?" Geraint was listening hard. He had heard about this before, from his Granddad. A couple of kids raised their arm.

"Jenn?"

"That's, like, Lancelot and Guinevere, Miss? S'that Clive Owen film, innit?" Jenn nudged the girl on her left, who giggled.

"Inspired, Jennifer. Anyone heard of Gawain and the Green Knight? No? Well, you really should know this, you know; there are loads of legends about Arthur based in Cheshire. None of you ever been to Alderley Edge?" "Well," Miss Deed continued with a sigh, walking to the window. "Cheshire is an unusual county, it's full of myths and legends. Partly that's to do with its position as a border county, just on the edge of Wales, which is one of the places scholars have suggested Arthur came from." She crossed the centre of the room, threading through desks. "A medieval poem talks of Gawain travelling on his quest from wild Wales to the hills of the border county. He meets a Green Knight in the wooded hillside and has to go through a series of tests. Some people have said that the hill Gawain crosses could be Helsby Hill itself. Anyone know what a Green Man is?"

Before he can stop himself, Geraint answers breathlessly, "It's an ancient nature symbol of a man, made of the forest and foliage, Miss. He's the symbol for death and rebirth. You can find figures of him on churches. I've seen them."

Miss Deed looked at him intently. James had turned round, his face hard and implacable.

"That's it, well done. It's exactly that, a symbol for death and resurrection, which the church used to symbolize the Reborn God. The Green Man's also a spirit of the woods and a mischievous figure in folk tales, a bit like Robin Hood," Miss Deed continued. "Over here", pointing across to the estuary, "this could be where Gawain crossed water in the poem and up there" - she pointed up to the left, to a space behind the blank classroom wall - "the sandstone cliff at Helsby Hill could be where he met the Green Knight. Of course, where we are sitting now would be all have been forested back then".

Geraint picks up his pace as he reaches the flat path snaking along the ridge of the hill. His breath comes more easily, as his legs have found a natural rhythm. It is still dense with trees and he stumbles over some tree roots in the sandy ground. Just to his left, the lights of the power plant begin to glow through the woods, like plankton catching light under water. He breathes in deeply: dog fox, ferns, the acrid scent of ivy stings his nostrils. He can smell the earth. He has no idea how long he has been running.

"Gawain?" snorted James. "That's a girl's name, Miss. Sure he wasn't a pansy? Sounds like Geraint, doesn't it? Or doesn't that sound more like Guinevere?" Miss Deed ignored him.

"Hey, Miss, isn't it true that you can still shoot a Welshman with a bow and arrow if you find him within the walls of Chester after dark?" He swivelled around in his chair to look at Geraint dead on. James bent his arms into the shape of an archery bow, stretched the shape back slowly, precisely into a perfect arch and then let it fly. "Thud, you're dead."

Geraint was in the garden with his Granddad. They were both digging in the vegetable plot, turning sods of clay soil over ready for the next crop. His Granddad was bent double over his spade. His brown weathered boots were thick with mud. He looked up at Geraint.

"Can you remember when we went to Alderley Edge with your Mum and Dad? Before ...." He hesitated. "Well, before the accident? Do you remember the caves of the sleeping knights? I thought we might go again this weekend. It's two year on now, you know." Geraint nodded agreement, without meeting his eye. "They were something else, those knights, weren't they, Geraint? Men of honour, dedicated to each other. All they had to rely on was friendship and their own courage." His Granddad's chest heaved and he carried on digging.

Geraint looked down at the ground, thinking of his parents. He felt blinded by the grains of soil. They seemed to separate before his eyes, shifting and squirming like a million tiny organisms.

He runs along the ridge as if he is nothing but air. His feet make barely an impression on the sandy ground. He is a blur of green, of woods and trees and wind. He is organic, he is a living thing. His heart is separate from his body, an organ pumping in front of him, urging him on.

He was heading for the school gates when James and three other lads sidestepped to cut him off. "Where're you going, silent boy? Girlie boy, eh?" James challenged him and pushed him backwards. Laughing, they moved in closer as he stumbled back. Geraint stepped forward, looked James right in the eye, keeping his voice low. "Just piss off!" - and he ran.

"Get him!" Their challenge hung in the air.

The trees are unravelling around him. The roots squirm across the ground and thrash at his ankles. They lash themselves around his arms, his knees, his chest. He feels the thin roots twist round his wrists and dig themselves into his veins. They pull him from tree to tree, relentlessly forward. He is part of the forest, the heart of the wood and his heart beats with pure courage.

It is dark when he reaches the edge of the wood. He is walking calmly towards the lights at the top end of the town. The woods open out into clearings and the sky hangs dark blue above him, splashed with stars. He walks slowly to the wooden gate at the bottom of the path and waits.

It takes an extra half an hour for James to arrive, his legs flailing with exhaustion. He stops, red-faced and straining for breath, as soon as he sees Geraint and bends down, his sweaty palms leaning on his thighs. He looks up at Geraint and nods. There is an understanding between them. Geraint nods back, turns away and heads for home, smiling.

CLEAN-UP BOY

Pauline Leung

"Hi, I'm Clean-Up Boy." I scowled at my scrawny reflection and tried again - this time in a deep bear growl, like Dad's. "Hi, I'm Clean-Up Boy, here to – um - clean up..."

Pete, the Clean-Up Boy! How pathetic is that? Everyone else gets to be proper superheroes. Why was I cursed to be the one to clean up after the fights? I didn't even have a cape. Obviously, I wasn't meant to be a superhero.

Oh-oh, my watch flashed. It's waterproof, tells what time it is in five countries and it warns me when I'm needed in the eternal fight against evil. I have to go. In the meantime, here's a flashback.

If Bonsai Kid (don't laugh, it's worse than it sounds; he miniaturizes everything in his path) hadn't zapped Charlie, the real Clean-Up Boy, with his cobbled together ray gun, Mr Impervious wouldn't have flown in front.

If Mr Impervious hadn't had an invulnerable chest, the ray wouldn't have rebounded and hit me. And I wouldn't have been standing in the line of fire if Dad hadn't accepted a contract with Lamme Studios in America. Mum's chin had wobbled at the news, so Dad arranged for us to go too, as "nine months is a ridiculously long time to be separated from your family".

If megastar Betty Beta-Jones hadn't insisted on Dad doing her make-up and lighting because, "he was the only artist in the whole universe to understand where she was at" (don't ask me; I'm just reporting), then the producer wouldn't have offered Dad squillions to work for him. And when you've got a mortgage and two - I mean, one

102

growing kid to support - you've got to take what comes. Even if it means uprooting to a country which lives in the past (America's about four hours behind).

So really, it was all Betty's fault I got hit by Bonsai's crummy laser. In one fateful moment, a twelve-year-old kid - so skinny, his family nicknamed him Ribster - was transformed into a skinny superhero, of sorts.

While Dad was busy plastering and airbrushing Betty and Mum was charming Tommy Deep, the lead, for his autograph, I decided to explore.

"Where are you going, Pete?" said Mum instantly.

"It's boring, watching paint dry," I whined. "I want to look around. Please, Mum, I promise not to go far."

"He'll be fine." Dad took my side. "This is a secure film set; what could possibly happen?"

So, armed with my pass, which just about gets me anywhere interesting without questions, I set off to explore the back of beyond: i.e. the unused units in the back lot - it was like a graveyard for obsolete sets. Brilliant.

I found a broken wooden sword and did my gladiator impression. "I am Peterus Maximus, son of Georgious Gregarious - defender of the weak, avenger of the slain ...

"Stop, Bonsai Kid," someone thundered, "you are surrounded!"

A weird kid with green hair and matching costume dashed past and clambered up over a broken monument. Must be a rehearsal, I thought, and followed.

Someone else cackled, "Take that, sucker!"

I heard a whooshing noise, like a vacuum cleaner sucking up a pillow by mistake. The boy said, "Oh, bother," before shrinking into nothing!

There was another whoosh, and I saw stars.

"What's that smell? Angelo, is that you?" said a mustachioed thin man.

"Fertilizer," retorted a caped man, "Bonsai must have put it in his ray gun. Listen, Mesmic, you call me 'Mr Impervious' when we're on duty. How many times do I have to remind you?"

Mesmic shrugged. "Mick, Michaelangelo - what's in a name?"

Mr Impervious frowned. "Was his hair green before?"

"Whom the Gods love dyes young," intoned Mesmic. He suddenly waved his hands in front of me like a mad conductor: "You vill forget - you haff no memory of vat has just occurred."

I looked at him blankly. What a weirdo!

Mesmic tossed his cape over his shoulders. "It's worked." He dropped his phony accent.

"You sure about that?" Mr Impervious didn't sound convinced.

Mesmic glared at him. "Have I ever been wrong?"

"Yeah."

"When?"

"When Crook Jaw pulled a faint and then tried to blackmail us by threatening to reveal our identities to the press - oh, and what about the time ...?"

"Okay, okay, and I suppose you've never slipped up, Mr Perfecto?"

While the two were busy arguing, I was slowly edging away as if I was sleepwalking.

"Hey, where's he going?" Mr Impervious snatched hold of my jumper.

"It's okay, let him leave. He can't see us," said Mesmic.

That stung. "Do you mind - I've got twenty-twenty vision." Me and my big fat mouth.

Mesmic went into his routine again, "You haff no memory - "

"Wow, look at that mess," I interrupted, knocking his hands away and pointing at the rubble - all that was left of the Roman Coliseum. Normally, I'm not so rude, but it's really annoying when someone is right in your face, practically poking your eyes with his abnormally long, blue, varnished nails.

I hate people demonstrating. You know the type: those who re-enact events like stabbing or strangling, trying to make it vivid - as if words are not enough. It's not funny. When Mark, our neighbour back home, jabbed at my chest, I belted him.

No sooner had I pointed than the broken bits of plaster pulled themselves together into Corinthian columns, as if I'd pressed rewind on a video.

"Wow," I gasped, "D-did you see that?"

"This has never happened before," Mr Impervious said, worriedly. His frown concertinaed right up to his kiss curl. "You know what this means, don't you?"

"What?" I didn't have a clue what he was talking about.

Mesmic grinned. He jumped and posed theatrically. "Ta-daah! You're our new Clean-Up Boy!"

"When you say, 'clean-up', you mean - what?" I asked.

"Clean-up as in cleaning up the mess that's left after saving the world." Mr Impervious flexed his muscles.

"Have we met before?" A strange cold thrill tickled the hairs on my neck. "You look a lot like Michael."

"I don't think so - who's Michael?" Mr Impervious said.

"Just someone I knew."

"We are all brothers," said Mesmic, smiling gently. "Part of the same team."

So that's how it all began. Mild mannered, bespectacled kid masked my alter ego: Clean-Up Boy. It wasn't the easiest of jobs. Superheroes are untidy; I mean, *really* untidy. As for villains—don't get me started. If they can wreck a subway, smash up a highway choked with cars and ignite a gas explosion in the sewers, they will. Even with my clean-up skills, it's still gross.

When Dad's contract finished and we went back to Britain, I thought that was it and I could hand in my notice. No such luck! My watch would flash in the middle of the night and off I'd zoom across the Atlantic. Once, I was in such a rush, I forgot to change. This was really embarrassing and Mr Impervious and Mesmic have never let me forget it. Anyway, prison-striped pyjamas aren't *that* funny. Now, I wear my costume beneath my normal clothes.

I like being a superhero, even a minor one. It's great fixing stuff up after it's been blown to smithereens. One of the perks when I'm in superhero mode is that my hair changes from forgettable-mouse-brown to a cool green.

I wish I had had this power when my brother disappeared, six years ago. Mikey hid me in a tree hollow and told me to be very quiet until he returned, because someone bad was following us. At the memorial service, I kept telling Mum Mikey was coming back, but she started crying.

It doesn't matter if no one remembers what we superheroes do; I know I've made a difference and that's what counts. I have my off days; who doesn't? I wouldn't change it, really. Once you start being a hero, there's no going back; you have to see it through. Someone's got to do it; why not me? The work's never finished; a new villain always replaces the old.

Right, I'm back now. You should have been there. We neutralized an atomic weapon - that was tough - then we captured a madman who wanted to take over the world and saved a little girl and her dog.

Mum shouted from downstairs, "Pete, have you cleaned up yet?"

"All the time," I want to reply, "all the time."

Clean-Up Boy

You think this is make-believe, don't you? Chew over this - next time you're out with your friends - maybe, walking across the road, and you suddenly feel you've done that before - chances are you just did. Five minutes earlier, a lorry had careered around the corner and shed its load of new cars. You were nearly history, but Mr Impervious saved you, Mesmic hypnotized everyone and I cleaned up the mess. You're welcome.

Memo: In case you're wondering what happened to Charlie - he's working in computers - literally. When your set goes on the blink, stop bashing the sides; it spoils his concentration.